DIGGING IT

**By Bunny Henderson
with Rebecca Lubow**

Publication design, photo restoration and illustration by Dennis Dickerson
www.respondgrafiks.com

URBAN FARMING
Global Food Chain®

This book is dedicated to our global family.

Urban Farming™ would like to extend a very special thanks to some of the wonderful people who have helped throughout the years including: Teretha Moore, Michael Travis, Joyce Lapinsky and Richard Lewis, Craig Kallman, Atlantic Records, Cherry Flowers, Eric Parrish, Chip and Kathleen Rosenbloom, Sister Dorothy Washington, Gail Carr, Beverlyn Hilton, Les Daggs, Antonia Bennett, Johanna Bennett, Latoris Shepherd, Edith Steanhouse, Joel Dorfman, Willie Sledge, Rasheed Neville, Prince, T.I., ROAR Management, Bubble Up Interactive, Roy Daggs, Kathy Adams, Tevis Foreman, Slice, Alnando Rodriguez, Toni Profera, Gary LeMel, Kent Seton & Associates, Susan Kilbride, the Beck family, the Moore family, Mary Monahan, Henry and Sarah Richardson and family, Denise Rich, Annette Jordan, Nile Rodgers and Nanci Hunt, Shakolad, Ken Abdo/Lommen & Abdo, Stacey Crawford, Marijane Mader, Jerry Soto, Daniel Assael, Robin Osler, Barry Kolsky and the countless others who have supported Urban Farming™.

The author would also like to thank: Donald Klein, Gayle Myers-Harbison and Gene Henderson

Second Edition
Published by Urban Farming™
Library of Congress Cataloging in Publication Data
Henderson, Bunny with Lubow, Rebecca
Digging It

ISBN 978-0-9823030-1-6

1. Gardening
Art Credits: Posters on pages i, 1, 9, 15, 28 and 89 courtesy of the United States Department of Agriculture. Photos on pages 1 and 17 courtesy of the Farm Security Administration, Office of War Information Photographic Collection, Library of Congress.

CONTENTS

INTRODUCTION

We are all the architects of our future and we are experiencing a paradigm shift in the way that we approach global challenges. Whether in good times or bad times, our world is changing to a new model that will become a way of life.

In the world of gardening, the global non-profit organization Urban  Farming™ has been on the forefront of this change. Urban Farming has been an active leader in promoting the multiple benefits of growing food in community or residential gardens. During World War II, nearly 20 million people planted Victory Gardens and they grew almost half of the produce supply in the United States.

If they were able do it back then without any of our current technological advantages, then we can do it now, on a larger scale. Urban Farming is doing just that. In 2012, we launched our *"Urban Farming 100 Million Families and Friends Campaign™,"* encouraging people to register their gardens and farms on the Urban Farming website and to become a part of the *"Urban Farming Global Food Chain®."* We intend to be the first generation to get rid of hunger. Through our *Urban Farming Coexistence Model™*, we also address: business growth, job creation, health and wellness, urban redevelopment, urban agriculture and global investment. We reach people who are unemployed, underemployed, laid off, malnourished, have unhealthy diets or are hungry. We also reach people who love to garden and love to give back!

We help empower people and create economically stable communities, and we start with a garden. Gardening produces healthy food, cuts down on food costs and relieves stress. This book is a great guide for people who are just starting out or who have been gardening for some time. It makes creating your own garden easy and fun! There are simple directions to guide you and helpful information about how to preserve your crop. There are even instructions on how to use your own produce to make teas and soothing oils.

The first garden step is to obtain a soil sample and have it tested for toxic elements. We suggest that you contact your local university extension office or SGS Mowers for information on the step-by-step soil sampling process. SGS Mowers: www.sgs.com.

Although there is a list of resources in this book from all over the United States and Canada, Urban Farming is global and we continue to expand our worldwide gardening tips and resources on our website. All of the proceeds from this book help to support the mission of Urban Farming, and by purchasing this book you are a part of the *Urban Farming Global Food Chain*®!
So dig in and don't forget to register your garden at: www.urbanfarming.org.

Thank you!

Taja Sevelle
Founder, Urban Farming

ii

PLAN YOUR PLOT

So you're going to plant a garden! The first thing you have to do is to find a good spot. Look for a place that gets at least six hours of sun a day and that has good drainage. If water tends to pool in the spot where you'd like to put your garden, either work the soil enough to improve the drainage *(more on this later)*, use raised beds, bring in soil to level the land, or terrace the plot. The original Victory Gardens of the 1940's were about 35 x 35 feet and we include plans for a garden of nearly that size in this book. We also have a plan for a smaller garden that should give you enough space to grow plenty of food to eat during the spring, summer and fall and to preserve for the winter. Of course, you can always adjust the measurements to fit your situation.

If your backyard doesn't have a space that fits the requirements, don't despair. Consider digging up part of your front yard to use as your garden, talk to your neighbors about sharing a space, or get in touch with your city government to find out if they have community gardens where you can rent a spot. And those of you who would love to grow things but don't have a backyard should see the section on Gardening in Containers. You'll be amazed at how much good food a window box can yield!

❧ *12' x 12' Sample Garden Plan* ❧

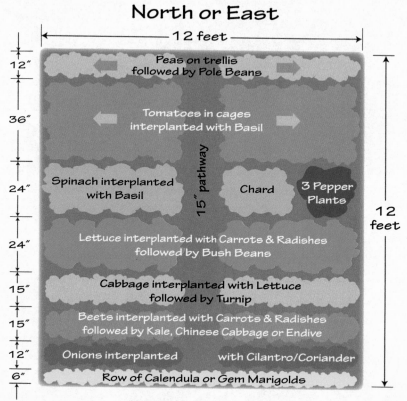

North or East

12 feet

12"

36"

24"

24"

15"

15"

12"

6"

Peas on trellis
followed by Pole Beans

Tomatoes in cages
interplanted with Basil

15" pathway

Spinach interplanted
with Basil

Chard

3 Pepper
Plants

12
feet

Lettuce interplanted with Carrots & Radishes
followed by Bush Beans

Cabbage interplanted with Lettuce
followed by Turnip

Beets interplanted with Carrots & Radishes
followed by Kale, Chinese Cabbage or Endive

Onions interplanted   with Cilantro/Coriander

Row of Calendula or Gem Marigolds

South or West

A word about the garden plans. These plans are drawn to scale. Even so, when you start to plant, use the measurements between the rows to wind up with a correctly scaled garden. Next, notice that the plans call for flowers inter-planted with the vegetables. These flowers are all beneficial to the vegetables they are near *(see companion planting on page 29)*, and they're also edible. The gem marigolds have a citrus flavor, the flowers and leaves of the nasturtiums have a peppery taste, and the calendula petals are faintly sweet. Use them in salads or eat them straight off the stem.

You see, too, that some crops are planted in the same row as others,

2

❧ 25' x 25' Sample Garden Plan ❧

North or East

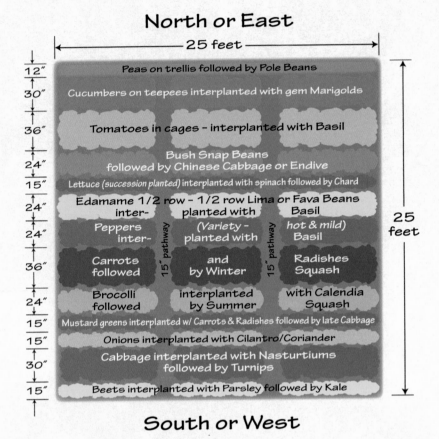

|← 25 feet →|

12"

Peas on trellis followed by Pole Beans

30"

Cucumbers on teepees interplanted with gem Marigolds

36"

Tomatoes in cages - interplanted with Basil

24"

Bush Snap Beans
followed by Chinese Cabbage or Endive

15"

Lettuce (succession planted) interplanted with spinach followed by Chard

24"

Edamame 1/2 row - 1/2 row Lima or Fava Beans
inter-   planted with   Basil

24"

Peppers   (Variety -   hot & mild)
inter-   planted with   Basil

36"

Carrots   and   Radishes
followed   by Winter   Squash

15' pathway   15' pathway

24"

Brocolli   interplanted   with Calendia
followed   by Summer   Squash

15"

Mustard greens interplanted w/ Carrots & Radishes followed by late Cabbage

15"

Onions interplanted with Cilantro/Coriander

30"

Cabbage interplanted with Nasturtiums
followed by Turnips

15"

Beets interplanted with Parsley followed by Kale

25 feet

South or West

after the first round of vegetables has been picked. This is called succession planting and on the plot diagram, it's indicated by the words "followed by." Succession planting makes better use of your space and allows you to have a variety of crops that mature at different times throughout the season. Just dig up the first crop, work the soil, and plant the new crop. Finally, remember that you can modify the garden to fit your needs. You can adjust the size according to how much space you have, keeping in mind that the larger your garden, the more profitable your return. Also, you can plant more or less of any of the recommended vegetables, depending on the tastes of your family.

GATHER YOUR TOOLS

Basic Gardening Tools

A spading fork. This is used to break up and aerate the earth.

A long spade with a flat bottom edge to dig the earth.

A long handled shovel with a pointed or rounded tip to get out rocks & move soil.

A steel rake to break up smaller clods of earth and to smooth out the garden.

A hand trowel with a pointed or rounded edge to dig holes for transplanting and for heavy-duty weeding.

A dandelion digger which has an 8 inch metal rod to get out weeds with taproots.

A clipper/pruner to cut vegetables from vines and remove dead branches.

Gardening gloves, string or twine, some stakes (old twigs can work for this).

A weeding hoe for weeding & loosening soil around the plants.

Your weeding hoe can be long handled if you want to weed standing up, or a hand hoe to weed while kneeling or sitting. A soil thermometer and scissors or a pocket knife are also handy.

 TIP **Check ebay (www.ebay.com) and Craigslist (www.craigslist.com) for possible tool bargains.**

Once you've chosen your location, you'll need to get some tools to change your spot of land into a garden. A gardener's tools become his friends. As silly as it might sound to someone who has never gardened, it doesn't take long to become attached to a particular trowel or shovel. The old saying, "You get what you pay for," applies to garden tools, and though it might be tempting to go for a cheap shovel or trowel, you're better off to spend a little more and buy tools that won't break when the work starts. When you shop for tools, forget plastic and invest in steel. Give special attention to the joint where the metal meets the wood to make sure it's strong. Hold tools in your hands before you buy them to make sure they fit your grip. Check to make sure that the rake, spade and shovel feel right to you. Do a little "air gardening" before you buy.

You can cut costs on buying the more expensive gardening equipment if you go in with your neighbors and all share in the cost, storage and maintenance of the tools.

You can't have a garden without your tools, so think of them as partners in this endeavor, and treat them accordingly. Caring for your tools is critical if you want them to last longer. Wipe off the blades of tools after you've been digging and put them back in the place you've made for them, whether it's in a tool shed, garage or closet. It's really tempting to just drop your tools in the garden when you're done digging, but take a few extra minutes to clean them and put them away even when you're dying to go in and get a glass of something cool to drink. Wrap a piece of brightly colored tape around your tool handles or spray with florescent paint so you can spot that trowel or clipper in your garden just in case you leave it there by mistake. And keep a towel in the tool shed so you can clean your tools every time you store them.

To keep your hand tools sharp over the winter, fill a bucket with sand, pour in some cooking oil, stick the tools blade-first into the bucket and leave them there until the robins return in the spring.

CHOOSE YOUR PLANTS

"Seed Catalog." Say those words to a gardener and watch the reaction. There are few greater pleasures than sitting around on a cold winter's day looking through seed catalogs and imagining your summer garden. You can expect most seed catalogs to list their seeds, show pictures of the mature plants, and give basic growing information. Some seed companies go way beyond the basics and are almost encyclopedic in the information they provide. Take time to read about the plants that appeal to you and always make sure that the seeds you choose will do well in the part of the country where you live. This means you must consider the type of soil you have and figure out the length of the growing season. The zone and frost charts on page 8 will help you do this.

There are almost always more seeds in a packet than you'll need for one season. Some seeds will keep for a couple of years, but most lose their viability, so think about sharing seeds with your neighbors or go to an online seed swapping site. You can buy seeds in garden, hardware and grocery stores, but to get full information about the plants, seed catalogs are the way to go.

Here are the web sites of a few very reputable seed companies whose catalogs will keep you spellbound for hours, if not days:

 Where to go to . . . __BUY SEEDS__

www.seedsofchange.com—They grow their own seeds and also sell fertilizers and small tools.

www.johnnyseeds.com—The seeds are tested and dependable. Informative web site.

www.territorialseed.com—Many of the seeds are organic. Highly recommended.

www.richters.com—Wonderful selection of herbs, some very unusual. Home of the Potmaker.

www.growitalian.com—Seeds from Italy. Great customer service. Call to speak directly to the owner, Bill.

www.growabbo.org—Vegetable and some flower seeds, grown on their farm. Web site only, no catalog yet.

www.rhshumway.com—Fun catalog with both standard and unusual vegetables and flowers.

www.botanicalgardens.com—Wide selection of vegetables, flowers and herbs. Web site only.

www.garden.org/seedswap—A forum for exchanging seeds with other gardeners.

Most vegetables in the garden are annuals, which means that the plants go through their entire life cycle in one season. They're seeds when they begin and when you pick them at the end of the season, their growing lives are over. Annuals usually can grow in any area unless they need a particularly long growing season, which would limit them to places with long, hot summers. Biennials grow for two years. During the first year, they grow and put out leaves, but they usually don't flower or fruit until the second year. After that, they die. Perennials are plants that die back in the winter but come back again and get bigger year after year. Not all perennials will grow in all areas because of differences in soil and temperature.

Even though annual vegetables will grow almost everywhere, you still need to know your zone and frost dates before you start to plant. First check the USDA Zone Map and figure out your zone at *www.usna. usda.gov/Hardzone/*— OK, now onto frost dates.

The last frost day comes before the first frost day, which can be confusing to people who are used to having first come before last, so let me explain. You just have to think in terms of the calendar year. The last frost of the year comes earlier *(in April, say)* than the first frost of the year *(in November)*. Many plants can't handle frost, so it's important to know the last frost date so you don't plant too early. Other plants need the soil to be a certain temperature before they go into the ground, and the ground temperature depends on the date of the last frost.

> *Be aware that your last frost day may occur earlier and your first frost day may be later than the chart indicates. You may have more days to grow your garden. Also, many micro-climates exist within each zone. Sometimes there are as many as 10 days difference in frost dates between towns that are only 15 miles apart. If you have questions, use this web site to find your local extension office. Contact the experts there and ask what they think. www.csrees.usda.gov/Extension/*

Almost every seed packet will tell you the time to plant in terms of the frost date. Here are those approximate dates. For exact information contact your extension office.

Zone	Last Frost Date	First Frost Date
1	June 15	July 15
2	May 15	August 15
3	May 15	September 15
4	May 15	September 15
5	May 15	October 15
6	April 15	October 15
7	April 15	October 15
8	March 15	November 15
9	February 15	December 15
10	January 31	December 15
11	Zone 11 has no frost!	

While we're at it, here's information on what constitutes a freeze:

Light freeze: 29° F to 32° F—kills tender plants, most others live.

Moderate freeze: 25° F to 28° F—most annuals will die and fruit blossoms will experience heavy damage.

Severe freeze: 24° F and colder—damage to many semi-hardy plants.

DECISIONS, DECISIONS, DECISIONS

Now that you've looked at the seed catalogs and you've chosen the plants that will grow in your zone, you need to decide how you want to approach the planting situation. One choice isn't better than another—it all depends on how much time you want to spend on the planting process. The easiest and quickest way to get plants is to buy seedlings. Another choice is to buy seeds and plant them directly in the ground. If you really want to test your growing skill, you can go with the third choice, which is to germinate seeds and grow your own seedlings. Let's look into the particulars of each option.

Sow the seeds of Victory!
plant &
raise
your own
vegetables

WRITE TO THE
NATIONAL
WAR GARDEN
COMMISSION—
WASHINGTON, D.C.
for free books on
gardening, canning
& drying.

"Every Garden a Munition Plant"

If you don't have the time or desire to plant seeds, and you didn't grow your own seedlings, then the best way to find plants is to go to your local farmers' market. The plants have been growing in greenhouses during the late winter so they'll be ready for you to plant in your newly prepared plot. There are many compelling reasons for buying seedlings from a local farmers' market. First, the plants that make it to the market will be strong and hardened off (*which means that they are used to the outside temperature fluctuations of the season*). Second, you know they're coming directly from the greenhouse to you. Third, the varieties will be appropriate to the area where you live, and finally, the farmer can answer your questions about the plant itself or planting in general.

Another place you can look for already-growing seedlings is at a local garden center. The people there will also be able to answer your questions and guide you to the plants you need. A reason to stay local rather than go to a chain is that locally grown plants are more likely to be in good condition. The downside to looking for seedlings at the market or garden center instead of ordering seeds from a catalog is that the vendors might not have the EXACT variety you're looking for if you have something very specific in mind, but if you're open to what's available, shopping for seedlings in your hometown is the way to get started.

If you choose to plant your own seeds, buy the packets, get them all together and then check the planting directions that begin on page 27.

The third choice, germinating your own seeds, is the most challenging and time consuming, but can also be the most rewarding. If you decide to germinate, be aware that you have to start your seeds weeks before they need to be planted outside. Because of this earlier start time, I'll talk about how to germinate seeds at this point in the book.

❧ *Germinate Some Seeds* ☙

Let's start with a guide that tells you when to germinate your seeds indoors to plant the right seedling on the right date. Each plant has its own best germination time and temperature, so don't put all the seeds on the heat mat at once. The chart at right provides both temperatures and times in the season to germinate the seeds. Determine your last frost date and plant accordingly. "Direct seed" means to plant the seed in either a paper or peat container that it will stay in until transplanting. When you direct seed, put regular potting soil in the bottom ⅔ of the container and germination soil in the top ⅓ and keep moist.

Write your last frost date here _____

Write your first frost date here _____

WHEN TO GERMINATE SEEDS INDOORS

Vegetable/ herb	When to Plant	Soil Temp.	Days to Sprout
Spinach	11 weeks before last frost	65	5
Lettuce	11 weeks before last frost	65	3
Sage	11 weeks before last frost	65	6
Kale	11 weeks before last frost	65	10
Oregano	11 weeks before last frost	65	5
Parsley	10 weeks before last frost	70	8
Cabbage	9 weeks before last frost	70	5-17
Peas	8 weeks before last frost	70	7–soak for 2 hrs. /direct seed
Mustard Greens	7 weeks before last frost	70	2
Endive	7 weeks before last frost	70	6
Peppers	6 weeks before last frost	77	6
Tomatoes	5 weeks before last frost	77	3
Chinese Cabbage	5 weeks before last frost	77	9
Basil	3-4 weeks before last frost	77	3
Beans	2–2 ½ weeks before last frost	80	3–direct seed
Edamame	2 weeks before last frost	80	3–direct seed
Squash	2 weeks before last frost	80	2–direct seed
Cucumber	2 weeks before last frost	80	2–direct seed

To germinate seeds in a professional way, you should get a heating mat with a thermostat that regulates the mat temperature and a stand to which you can attach two or three 40 watt grow lights. The mats range from $25 to $75, the thermostats go for around $30, and the grow lights cost about $10 each. You can get everything from a garden supply store or a hardware store. Here are a few places where you can order heating mats and thermostats.

 Where to go to . . . <u>FIND HEATING MATS</u>

www.charleysgreenhouse.com—Professional mats and thermostats.
www.botanical.com/hydro/propagation/cloning—Less expensive choices.
www.parkseed.com—Smaller mats with built-in heat.
www.growerssupply.com—Professional mats and thermostats.

TIP *If you want to be more down-home about germination, you can use a heating pad and a lamp, but the results will be more predictable with the mat, thermostat and grow light.*

One thing you have to do whether you go professional or down-home is to use germination mix for germinating your seeds. This mix is much lighter than regular potting soil which makes it easier for the seeds to establish roots. You can order germination mix from many seed catalogs or get it at a garden center.

Garden centers and the web sites that sell heat mats also sell special black plastic containers with clear covers that are meant for seed germination, but people have been success-
ful using egg cartons and other small containers for growing seeds. Seed companies often sell containers made of peat or manure *(dried and de-stunk)*, but I've found that these don't disintegrate as well as those you can make

yourself of newspaper. You'll find a tool called a Potmaker in many seed catalogs, but since it was invented by Otto Richter, I encourage people to get it from the source at *www.richters.com*. Making the newspaper pot involves wrapping a four-inch strip of newspaper around the wooden spool-like top and pressing the spool into a round wooden plate. Once the three-inch newspaper pot is filled with moist soil, it remains remarkably strong. It also allows the roots to grow right through the paper, which is very good for the plant. When it comes time to transplant, you can either peel about an inch away from the top part of the paper cup, or plant the whole thing in the ground, where the paper will disintegrate.

Whichever type of container you use, moisten the germination mix to the consistency of a sponge that has been wrung out before you put it in the planting container. The mix should stick together when you squeeze it, but it should not drip. When you have the mix at this consistency, put it in your container.

Get germinating mix to the right consistency by filling a large mixing bowl with mix and adding water one or two cups at a time. Mix with your hands after each addition of water until you get it right.

Follow the directions on the seed packet for how deep to plant the seed, make the hole with a pencil point, drop in the seed, cover it with mix and then cover the entire container with either household plastic wrap or the cover that came with the plastic container. Then put it on the heat source under the grow light. The goal here is to create a little greenhouse with plenty of humidity to keep the seed growing. Make sure the soil stays moist, but not wet. You can accomplish this with a spray bottle filled with water rather than a big watering can.

Keeping track of germinating seedlings is like waiting for a package in the mail. You know the package is going to arrive, but you don't know exactly when. After checking the soil where the seeds are planted for a couple of days, you'll develop an eagle's eye for spotting the tiniest of sprouts. I've been known to cheer out loud when I see the first little shoots come up. You'll probably feel this way, too, but be careful about how much noise you make, because people have a tendency to make fun of those who get over-excited about the germination of a seed. Once the seeds come up and are about ¾"–1", take them off the heating mat, remove the plastic cover and place them two to three inches below a grow light. If the light is any further away from the top of the plant than those two or three inches, the seedling will be leggy, meaning that the stem is too long to support the leaves. It's very discouraging to have a new little seedling flop over because it was a few inches too far from its light source.

At first many seedlings look alike, but you'll see that the second set of leaves that your seedling grows, called the true leaves, will have the same shape as the leaves of the mature plant. When two sets of the true

True Leaves

leaves have come in, you can move the plant to a warm window. If it's in its own container, leave it there until it's time to plant. If you planted many seeds in a larger container, you need to move them out of the container, which you can do by digging them out with a small plastic grapefruit divider. Place them into small individual pots filled with regular potting soil. Water the seedlings when they get dry and let them grow while you prepare the soil outside.

PREPARE THE SOIL

D irt is dirt, right? Well, not exactly . . . gardeners used to tell me that the quality of your plants depend on the quality of your soil. I never believed them until I threw some compost into one of my gardens and saw the difference between the plants that grew in that garden and those that grew in the other. All dirt is not equal, and it's absolutely true that the time you spend in improving your soil will be rewarded in the size and health of your plants. A side benefit of working the soil is that it just makes you feel good, taking you back to the mud-pie days of childhood.

Groundwork for Victory
GROW MORE IN '44

The first thing you need to do to get the soil ready for planting is to dig up the earth. If the area you're digging has lots of weeds, do yourself a favor and throw the weeds out rather than just turning them over in the soil. If you leave them, they will rise from the dead to haunt you and your plants. The ideal situation is to dig it down 12 inches—18 inches is even better—so you have a deep bed of loose soil. The soil will eventually pack down some with time and weather, but loosely packed soil makes it easier for the roots to breathe. If you're up to it, use a shovel (*the ones with the pointed tips are most effective*) or a spading fork; if your shovel wielding days are over, then use a tiller. You can buy a tiller for between $350 and $1000 depending on the type or you can rent one for around $45 to $60 a day. In my opinion, this is money well spent (*well, not if you're using a window box*)!

An important thing to know about the soil that you're digging up is whether it's acid or alkaline. Soil is rated on a pH (*potential of hydrogen*) scale and its number affects the way certain plants grow. The scale runs from 0 to 14 with 7 being neutral. Soil with a high pH (*7.5 to 14*) is alkaline and with a low Ph (*0 to 6.5*) is acid. Some plants, like hydrangea, for

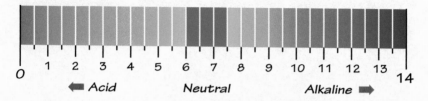

0   1   2   3   4   5   6   7   8   9   10 11 12 13   14

← *Acid*   *Neutral*   *Alkaline* ➡

example, love acid soil. Others, like lilacs, do best in alkaline. For most vegetables it's a good idea to have the soil in the neutral range *(6.0 to 7.5)*. To find out what type of soil your area has, the best thing to do is to call your local county extension office and ask them. It's possible to do soil tests, and you can bring a sample of your soil into the extension office *(see web site on page 8)* to find out exactly what pH your backyard is. Once you know the pH level of your soil, you can adjust it. Use lime to get acid soil more toward the pH you need for vegetables and add sulphur to alkaline soil to get it closer to the 7.0 number.

The next thing you need to do is to figure out whether you have clay, loam or sandy soil. This is not a hard thing to do. Clay is very dense and sticks together when it is wet and you press it in your hand. Sandy soil doesn't hold its shape when pressed and will fall through your fingers. Loam is soil that sticks together when you press it in your hand, but that  will crumble when you rub it between both hands. The density of the soil affects the way it holds moisture, which in turn affects the roots. Roots will rot or suffocate in too much moisture and dry up with too little, so the goal is to get soil that is loam. If you have loam where you want to plant your garden, do a dance of joy. If you have clay or sandy soil, you can improve the consistency by adding peat moss, sawdust or manure. If you don't get to the ideal consistency for your first garden, don't fret too much, but the crumbly soil is your ideal goal so keep adding those amendments every year.

Now that your soil is at the right pH level and getting to the right consistency, the next thing you do is enrich it with compost. This will improve the texture and the nutritional composition of the soil. Compost is basically a collection of decomposed organic matter and if you've ever walked in a forest and felt the soft earth under your feet, you were walking on natural compost. Compost happens when organic matter containing carbon and nitrogen is mixed with water and oxygen allowing bacteria to decompose the organic material. As this material decomposes, it produces heat and creates a nutrient-rich mixture. OK, that's your science lesson for the day. Adding compost to your soil is the best thing you can do for the future of your garden.

You have a couple of options with compost. The first is to buy it at a gardening center. If this is your first garden, you'll have to buy the compost to get started because it takes a while to make it—anywhere from two weeks to a year depending on what you use to make the compost. Try to get organic compost—you can get sheep manure, cow manure, mushroom compost or a mixture. Your second option is to buy compost from a farmer or co-op. Check in your phone book, call your extension office, or ask the farmers at your local farmers' market for resources. When you get the compost locally, you know your source and you can also ask direct questions about its make-up.

If you plan early enough, you can make your own compost, which is better than buying it because you know what's in it, you can feel good about making it, and it's virtually free! This doesn't mean that you have to go out and buy livestock; in fact, making your own compost is as easy as throwing your food scraps into a composter instead of into the garbage.

If you or someone in your family likes to do it yourself, here are directions for four very basic composters.

The first three composting plans don't involve building—just moving dirt. Before you start, make sure your city doesn't have rules against open compost heaps. To find out, call your city's environmental control office.

Do it now, here's how . . .
MAKING A COMPOST BIN

The first plan involves piling up the compost material on a three inch base of twigs and leaves and following the composting directions on page 21.

For the second plan, dig a 12 by 12 inch hole, put a couple of inches of twigs on the bottom and then follow the composting directions on page 21. A 12 x 12 inch compost heap isn't going to be enough to work into a huge garden, but it will get you started because it should ripen within a couple of months. You can keep making it and adding it to your garden throughout the year.

The third plan is basically the same as the second, but instead of making a 12 x 12 inch hole, you dig a hole big enough for a plastic garbage can with a lid that locks. Cut the out the bottom of the can and put it in the hole with about 12 inches of the can above the ground. Put in a two to three inch layer of twigs and follow the compost directions on page 21. Since this compost pile is enclosed by the locking lid, it should meet any composting requirements that your city might have.

The fourth composter is made from hardware cloth or chicken wire with a one or two inch mesh. If you're going to leave the composter in one place, build it around wooden or metal posts. If you want to be able to move it or lift it up to get to the bottom of the pile, leave the posts out.

Take a 10 foot length of the wire and bend back three inches of the rough cut edges. Stand the wire on edge and shape it into a three foot circle. Tie the two ends together at four inch intervals with heavy wire that you twist with a pair of pliers. You've just made a wire composter!

Always make sure the top of the compost pile has a little indentation in it to keep the water from running down the sides.

Where to go to . . . FIND COMPOST BIN DIRECTIONS

Here are a few web sites that have more detailed directions for making compost bins:

www.extension.missouri.edu/xplor/agguides/hort/
An outstanding site—Directions for many types of bins.
www.lowes.com/lowes/lkn?action=howTo&p=LawnGarden/compostBin
Complete directions for a wooden bin.
www.backyardgardener.com/compost/index—Directions for seven different types of bins.

If you'd like to skip the building and go directly to making the compost, then you can buy a composter. There are a few different types, and it's best to compare them before buying.

You can buy stationary composters of different sizes and shapes. They're relatively inexpensive *($100 to $150)* but some people have problems with turning the compost and getting the finished product out of the bin.

Another type of composter is the compost tumbler. These are usually round or oval shaped and come with a handle that you use to turn the entire bin to allow the compost to mix. The tumblers are usually more expensive *($180 to $600)* than the stationary bins, but they make the job of turning the compost easier.

The third type of composter is the worm compost bin, or vermicomposter. These are usually a stack of smaller bins about 12 inches square which cost from $90 to $245. The organic material is put in the top bins with the worms and comes out the bottom bin as compost and worm castings. The thought of this might make some people run away screaming, but worm bins are convenient because they get rid of the necessity to turn the compost and they also makes it possible for people who don't have the space for a large composter to still be able to make their own.

The latest composting innovation is the indoor composter that works by itself to compost kitchen waste. All you have to do is put the waste into the machine, which looks similar to a trash compactor, and turn it on. As you might expect, you pay for convenience. These composters run around $300.

Here are some web sites that sell composters and also give you more information about composting in general.

 Where to go to . . . <u>BUY COMPOSTERS</u>

www.composters.com—Different types of bins plus composting supplies.

www.growerssupply.com—Larger tumbling composters.

www.peoplepoweredmachines.com/composter—Good information. Top of the line bins.

www.gardeners.com—Good variety. Info on choosing composters.

www.compostbins.com/compost-bins—Big choice. Also has info on how to choose a bin.

www.smithandhawken.com—Different varieties of composters.

BEFORE YOU ACTUALLY MAKE COMPOST

Collect organic materials that are high in carbon and/or nitrogen.

Brown Materials—Items that are high in carbon, which are referred to as "brown" or "dry" materials, are wood ashes, tea bags, coffee grounds, bark, paper towels and bags, shredded cardboard, corn stalks, leaves, newspaper, peanut shells, peat moss, pine needles, sawdust, stems and twigs, hair, straw and vegetable stalks. Shred paper products and break up other materials into small pieces.

Green Materials—Materials high in nitrogen are referred to as "green" or "wet". They include alfalfa, algae, clover, egg shells, old plants, grass clippings, hay, hedge clippings, fruit peelings and cores, used hops, manure from herbivorous animals (not small pets or humans), seaweed, uncooked vegetable scraps and weeds if they have not gone to seed.

Once you have your bin, whether you made it yourself or bought it, you're ready make compost. Put the bin in a spot that you can reach with a water supply. Compost will break down and decay faster if the compost heap is placed in a shady location.

Do NOT use coal ash, meat, fish or dairy products or any cooked food. Also avoid any synthetic chemicals, chemically treated wood, colored paper or diseased plants.

Do it now, here's how . . .
MAKING COMPOST

Layering is the key to good compost. Have a good supply of both brown and green organic material at hand. First put down a three to five inch layer of brown dry material followed by a one inch layer of garden soil or compost sprinkled with a couple of handfuls of lime and fertilizer. Wet very lightly with either a watering can or the fine spray of a hose mister. If you would like to be the person who puts the "p" in compost, then you can urinate on the pile—no joke. It's just one more way to save on your water bill. Repeat the layers, but this time use a three to five inch layer of green wet material, and an inch of soil or compost followed by the lime and fertilizer and mist again. Repeat the layering and misting until the bin is full. A brown dry layer should be on top. Be careful not to over-water the layers. Let the pile sit for 10 days to two weeks and then take your spading fork and turn the material so the whole batch gets oxygen. Keep turning every 10 to 14 days and water lightly when you see the compost beginning to get dry. Compost can take anywhere from two weeks to a year to "ripen." You'll know it's done when the middle of the pile has cooled down and the batch looks dark and crumbly. What you just read is the Very Short Version of Composting—for more detailed information on the composting process check out the sites on the following page:

Where to go to . . . GET INFO ON COMPOSTING

www.composting101.com—Good basic info, from bins to monitoring moisture.

www.compostinfo.com—Easy to understand steps.

www.organicgardening.com—Basic compost directions.

www.compost-info-guide.com—Six easy steps to composting.

www.journeytoforever.org—A green site with detailed compost information.

RAISED BEDS

Kings and queens used to sleep in raised beds, and now your vegetables can, too. In a regular garden, the soil is dug up and enriched where it is and plants are put directly into the ground. In a raised bed, the earth is prepared as for a regular garden, then more soil is added inside wooden frames that rest on the ground. With raised beds the drainage is better, the fertilizer lasts a little longer, the soil warms up earlier in the season, and there's less bending for you when you weed. On the other hand, roots dry out faster, the soil may be a little more difficult to cultivate and it can be harder to rotate the crops every year. You also have to spend time and money to build the beds. As with almost every decision a gardener has to make, the choice depends on personal preference. I like raised beds for annuals because it's easier to enrich the soil every year and the fact that the soil gets warmer faster makes it possible for me to put in my vegetables a few days earlier in the season. On the other hand, I plant perennials in the ground where they have room to grow. The choice is yours.

If you consider the pros and cons of raised beds and decide that you'd like to have them, you have two options—you can buy raised bed kits from a garden supply store or you can make them yourself. The kits run from $44 to over $600 depending on the size and complexity of the beds. If you make your own eight by eight foot bed, you can expect to spend about $20 on lumber *(four eight foot landscaping timbers and one eight foot 4"x 4" piece of lumber)* and about $5 on a pound of #12 galvanized nails. To save money, make your own. How's that for an obvious conclusion?

 Where to go to . . . <u>BUY RAISED BEDS</u>

www.gardeners.com—Kits of wood, plastic, fieldstone. Garden info.

www.raised-garden-beds.com—Kits made of red cedar. Landscape plans on web site.

www.farmtek.com—Kits of composite lumber.

www.growerssupply.com—A good choice of kits including anchor joints and plastic lumber.

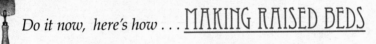 *Do it now, here's how . . .* <u>MAKING RAISED BEDS</u>

Buy four landscaping timbers and cut them to the size of the bed you want. You can also use railroad ties, but they can be hard to cut. If you go the railroad route, make sure the ties are not treated with creosote because it will hurt the plants. You can leave the soil under the bed undisturbed, but it's better if you dig it up to a depth of three to four inches. Turn it and mix it with compost. Take an eight foot 4" x 4", cut it into four pieces, and put one piece at each corner of the bed. Hammer the pieces into the soil, leaving enough board above the soil to attach to the landscaping timbers. This will stabilize the bed. Build up the height of the bed to six, eight or 12 inches, making sure the boards are securely attached to each other with #12 galvanized nails. Fill with topsoil mixed with compost, remembering to leave one to two inches of space on the top of the bed. You're done!

 Other materials you can use for framing are cinder blocks, rocks, bricks or redwood. Save money by buying recycled lumber or getting scrap from construction sites.

GARDEN IN CONTAINERS

You can still have a garden even if you live in an apartment or condo by using containers. If you have a balcony or a deck that gets sun for six hours a day, buy large pots or planters at your local garden supply store, order them from Earthbox *(www.earthbox.com)* or look for them on the web sites listed under seed catalogs and raised beds. Plastic containers tend to hold water longer than clay, but clay is more porous and lets the plants breathe easier. I like clay pots because they look more natural to me. Wooden barrels or half-barrels make good containers for tomatoes and other vining crops such as cucumbers. The most important thing about the containers is that they must have a drainage hole in the bottom, otherwise the roots can rot due to standing water. If you see a container that you really love that doesn't have a drainage hole, then put two to three inches of small gravel in the bottom to allow the water to drain out of the soil. The container depth should be almost equal to the height of the full-grown plant, so you're better off going for more narrow and deep containers rather that shallow and long containers for plants that are going to be over 18 inches tall. You can plant a short variety of carrots in a deep container, but don't try potatoes or other large root crops if you're a container gardener.

If you are planting in containers, you obviously can skip the digging and go directly to filling your containers with potting soil. You can buy potting soil at any garden center, but part of the joy of gardening is getting your hands dirty, and you can do this by making your own potting mixture. The major ingredients of most potting soils are peat moss, *(retains moisture)*, vermiculite *(retains moisture and releases it at a later time)*, perlite *(makes the mixture lighter and easier to drain)*, and compost, *(contains nutrients and releases them)*. Sometimes fertilizer is added to the mix. With this information, you can choose from the recipes at right:

24

Do it now, here's how . . .
MAKING POTTING SOIL

- ◆ 2 parts packaged potting soil
- ◆ 1 part vermiculite
- ◆ 1 part peat moss
- ◆ Slow release 10-10-10 fertilizer, amount dependent on directions on bag

———————— OR ————————

- ◆ 1 part potting soil,
- ◆ 1 part vermiculite
- ◆ 1 part peat moss

———————— OR ————————

- ◆ 1 part compost
- ◆ 1 part potting soil
- ◆ 1 part builder's sand

———————— OR ————————

- ◆ 1 part peat moss
- ◆ 1 part perlite
- ◆ 1 part compost
- ◆ 1 part potting soil
- ◆ Slow release 10-10-10 fertilizer, amount dependent on directions on bag

———————— OR ————————

- ◆ 2 parts peat moss
- ◆ 1 part sand
- ◆ ½ part perlite
- ◆ ½ part potting soil
- ◆ Osmocote fertilizer—2 cups to a 4 gallon bucket

You can make your own fertilizer by mixing together equal parts of:
- ◆ dolomitic limestone
- ◆ soybean meal
- ◆ greensand   (these are all available from garden centers)
- ◆ rock phosphate
- ◆ kelp powder
Add 1 cup of this fertilizer to each 8 cups of potting soil

You can mix the soil in a big plastic tub, or even in your kitchen sink.

If you really want to get with the program, you can make your own compost with an indoor vermicomposter. The idea of a worm apartment in your home or on your balcony might be a little disgusting at first, but when you think of it, worms are great pets. They don't need shots or licenses, you don't have to take them to the vet or out for walks, and they produce great compost that will make your vegetables fat and happy. If you're planting in containers, check the Plant Profiles on page 30, make a planting calendar, and fill your pots right before you're ready to put in either the seeds or seedlings. Follow the fertilizing directions in each Plant Profile. Container plants have to be watered more often than plants in the ground. To check to see if your plants need water, use the knuckle method—stick your finger in the soil and if it's dry down to the spot between your first and second down knuckle, it's time to water. When you do water your plants, pour it on until the water comes out the bottom of the pot. This will encourage root growth and increase times between waterings.

WHAT SIZE CONTAINERS FOR MY PLANTS?

Guidelines for the best-sized containers for different plants:

◆ *Bush beans, snap beans, lima beans, beets, cabbage, and Chinese cabbage*—one plant per five gallon container.

◆ *Carrots, radish*—two or three rows in a five gallon container that's at least 12 inches deep.

◆ *Cucumber*—One plant in a one gallon container with a little trellis for support.

◆ *Lettuce, onions, spinach, kale*—one row with four or five inch spaces between plants per five gallon container.

◆ *Peppers, summer squash*—one plant with support per two gallon container.

◆ *Tomatoes*—one cherry variety in a five gallon container/ two regular varieties in a 20 gallon container.

◆ *Herbs*—Plant in a zigzag row, four inches of space each way between each plant in a five gallon container.

If you want more plants, either buy more or bigger containers.

PLANT YOUR VEGETABLES

You've planned. You've prepared. Now you're ready to plant! Before you start to plant, stop for a minute and look at the seeds that you hold in your hand. In each one of those tiny seeds is an entire plant. Be amazed. One of the priceless benefits of growing a garden is to be able to take part in the daily miracles that nature constantly provides.

Now, let's get to the business of growing your garden.

❧ *Planting Seeds* ❧

If you decide to plant seeds directly rather than germinate them early or buy seedlings, here's how to do it. Make sure you line out the rows before you start. An easy way to do that is to put sticks on each end of every row that you're going to plant. Run a string between the two sticks at each row, then take the back of a rake, hoe, or even a pencil, and press a line into the earth under the string. The depth of the line will depend on how deep the seeds need to be planted. The exact depth should be on the seed packet but the rule of thumb is that seeds need to be buried to a depth of twice their size. Very small seeds can be sprinkled on top of the soil and pressed in.

To put the seeds in the ground, you can shake them from your hand or buy special seeders that are sold in some seed catalogs. Once the seeds are in the row, cover them to the right depth with the soil that was pushed aside by the back of the hoe, and water the garden with a very light sprayer to the depth of two to three inches. When the seedlings start coming up, which will vary depending on what you planted, thin them according to the directions in the Plant Profiles. When you thin plants, you pull out any seedlings that are growing closer than the recommended spacing in the Plant Profiles.

 Put small seeds in a salt shaker whose shaker holes have been enlarged with an awl and sprinkle onto the ground.

It's very tempting to leave all the seedlings in the ground. Some people have told me that they feel like murderers when they pull up the teeny plants, but if you don't thin them, you'll have a bunch of very small, puny plants instead of a few large, lush ones.

> **TIP** *You can use the pulled-up seedlings in salads, or you can also eat them straight out of the ground. Actually, you owe it to yourself to try this. It's amazing that no matter how small the seedling, it will taste like the mature vegetable.*

❧ *Planting Seedlings* ☙

The plants that you buy as seedlings should already be hardened off. Hardening off means exposing seedlings to the outdoors a little at a time. Think of it as toughening up the little sheltered plants so they'll be able to make it in the natural environment of the garden. If you've grown your seedlings from seeds, you can harden them off by taking them outside every day for about 10 days before you're ready to plant them. On the first day, bring them out after the sun is up for about two hours and back in before it goes down. Leave the plant out for longer times each day, and about three days before you're ready to plant, leave them out all day and all night. Use your judgment here, because if you have an unexpected cold snap during those last three days, you'll have to bring the plants in for that night.

When you're ready to plant your first batch of seedlings, work fertilizer into the soil. See Plant Profiles for the exact amount and type of fertilizer to use. Before you plant, dip the seedling, container and all, in a mixture of one gallon of water and ¼ cup of vitamin B1 or liquid kelp. This mixture stimulates the roots and gives the plant a little something to snack on. You can get both the kelp and the vitamin B1 at garden stores.

20

I prefer kelp because I can use it as a spray for the seedling leaves when they get to be about three inches high.

If you're using peat or paper, put the entire pot into the ground. If the plants are in plastic pots, loosen the roots if they're tightly packed and place the seedling in a hole that's just a little bigger than the plant. Pour some of the root stimulator mixture around each newly planted seedling once the soil is packed in around it.

❧ Companion Planting ❧

Do you remember the magnetism between Danny and Sandy in the movie *Grease*? What about Romeo and Juliet? Well, there's chemistry between plants as well as people, and gardeners can take advantage of that phenomenon. Companion planting is the practice of planting certain crops together in order to have them improve each other's growth and discourage disease. On the other hand, certain plants don't get along and it's important to plant them far from each other. The garden plans on pages 2 and 3 use the principle of companion planting.

A few examples of plant chemistry are:

Basil and marigolds help almost anywhere in the garden. Basil intensifies the flavor of all vegetables, especially lettuce and tomatoes, while marigolds promote growth. Both of these keep insects away from other plants.

Onions keep pests away from lettuce, cabbage, carrots and beets, but inhibit growth if they're planted near peas and beans.

Nasturtiums repel harmful bugs from cabbage, radishes, squash and beans.

Broccoli does better if it's planted near beets, carrots, and calendula.

To find out more about plant companionship so you can use this green chemistry, go to *www.attra.ncat.org/attra-pub/complant.html*

To dry herbs and flowers, cut them early in the morning and make a bunch of five or six stems. Wrap a rubber band around the stems and hang them upside down over a hanger. Place the hanger in a cool, dark closet for a week or two.

PLANT PROFILES

⅏ *The Vegetables in Your Garden* ⅋

The vegetables in the profiles are limited to those plants recommended for the *Digging It* garden. They're listed in alphabetical order. Once you decide on your garden plan, check out the Plant Profiles to find when, where and how to plant each vegetable. After you read through all the profiles, make a calendar of planting times to use as your guide throughout the season.

> **TIP** *Here's how to know when to plant each of the vegetables. Get a piece of paper and write the last frost date for your area at the top. You can copy this from where you wrote it down on page 10. Now list all the vegetables you're going to plant in your garden. As you read through the Profiles, note how many weeks before or after the frost date that the seed or seedling should be planted. Now you can copy the dates from your list to a calendar, and you're set for the season.*

You'll be managing and experiencing your garden in three major phases, so I'll give you the information about each recommended plant according to those phases. First you PLANT the vegetable, then you CARE for it and finally you HARVEST it. We mention fertilizing, weeding, and pest control in each of the Care sections of the Plant Profiles. Detailed information on these three topics can be found starting on pg. 71.

OK, now. Here we go!

BEANS

Just so you know, January 6 is National Bean Day. Now that you're an Official Home Gardener, you might want to mark it on your calendar before we get on to learning about beans. There are three major types of beans: snap, shelling and dry. The snap beans are cooked whole, the shelling beans, such as lima and fava, are taken out of the pod before the beans are hard, and dry beans are left on the vine to dry, shelled, and then used for soups and stews. To get even more detailed, snap beans grow both as bush beans and pole beans. Who would have thought beans could be so complex!

ᔑᓄ *Snap Bush Beans* ᘛ

◆ *PLANT*—Make sure the soil is over 60° when you plant bean seeds. This is about one to two weeks after the last frost.*_____. Seedlings can go out at this time also. Beans like soil that is slightly acidic, in the 5.5-6.5 range, so you can adjust your soil accordingly. Plant the seeds about one inch deep and about three inches apart. Water. Bush snap beans don't need any trellis support as they grow.

◆ *CARE*—Mulch *(see page 73)* around the beans and make sure the soil around them doesn't dry out. If you see any insects or fungus on the plants, spray them—or you can pick them off if they are beetles. No extra fertilization is necessary for beans.

31

◆ *HARVEST*—Bush snap beans are ready to be harvested when the seeds are small and the pods are firm, about two weeks after the seeds start to form. Pick carefully to keep from pulling the branch off with the bean.

෨ *Snap Pole Beans* ෪

◆ *PLANT*—Pole beans have the same planting and care directions as bush beans, except that the pole beans grow into vines, so they need a trellis to grow up. You create a simple trellis by making a teepee of long sticks, stretching rows of string between two wires, or by installing a section of metal fencing next to where the beans will be growing. As the seedlings begin to grow, train them to the trellis. Place your trellis in a spot that won't shade any of the other plants in the garden.

◆ *CARE*—see Snap Bush Beans.

◆ *HARVEST*—While bush beans tend to mature all around the same time, pole beans are ready to harvest at different times throughout the season. Pick the beans when the pods are firm and you can feel the little seeds inside. If the pods of the beans are very hard, let them grow a little longer.

෨ *Green Shelling Beans (Lima and Fava)* ෪

◆ *PLANT*—Shelling beans have the same planting and care directions as bush beans, except that the soil temperature should be at least 65°. This makes the planting date about two to three weeks after the last frost. *_____.

◆ *CARE*—see Snap Bush Beans

◆ *HARVEST*—Shelling beans are bush beans, so they'll all mature around the same time. Pick them when the pods have turned color and you can feel the fully formed beans inside the pod.

ɰ *Dry Shelling Beans* ଓ

◆ **PLANT**—see Green Shelling Beans

◆ **CARE**—See Snap Bush Beans

◆ **HARVEST**—Dry shelling beans dry on the vine. That's probably why they're called DRY shelling beans. You'll know it's harvest time when most of the leaves have fallen off the vine and the pods are dried out and beginning to open. Don't pick the beans until you can hear them rattle in the shell.

BEETS

For those interested in trivia—during Roman times, beet juice was used as an aphrodisiac. Coming back to the 21st century, the beet is called a root vegetable because the main part grows underground. Because it's a root vegetable, compost should be worked into the ground down to at least three to four inches to make the beet's life easy when it grows. It's good to do this for the whole garden, but definitely do it for the beets. A little beet doesn't have much of a chance against a big rock, so make sure the beet patch is cleared of obstacles. A good thing about beets is that you can eat both the greens and the root—and you can dye material with the water that's left from cooking. A multi-talented vegetable, indeed!

◆ **PLANT**—Plant beets one week to 10 days before the last frost date. *_____ The soil temperature should be from 55° to 65°. Beets like neutral soil *(7.0 pH)*, so if you've amended your garden to reach that level, you're all set. Root vegetables don't do well as transplants, so sow seeds directly. Put some liquid kelp in water and soak the seeds the night before you plant. Plant them about ½ inch deep and one inch apart, then cover them with a very

33

light layer of compost or germination mix. Water. When the beet greens are three inches tall, thin the plants so they're about four inches apart. The thinnings are great in a salad! Beets can be planted again in July if you'd like a fall crop.

- ◆ *CARE*—Keep the plants moist. Again, mulch works well for this. Once beets are planted in compost rich soil, they don't need to be fertilized. If you see harmful insects on the beet greens, spray them with an organic pesticide.

- ◆ *HARVEST*—Beets will be ready to harvest in about 55 to 65 days after planting. Loosen the soil around the top of the beet and pull gently on the greens.

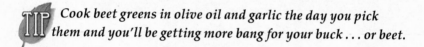

Cook beet greens in olive oil and garlic the day you pick them and you'll be getting more bang for your buck . . . or beet.

BROCCOLI

Probably the hardest vegetable to spell—are there two "c"s or two "l"s? No matter how you spell it, broccoli is a great vegetable for the garden because it's high in nutrients and easy to grow.

- ◆ *PLANT*—Broccoli is a cool weather crop, which means you can get both a spring and a fall crop if you want. In the spring, instead of seeds, use seedlings which can be put out three weeks before the last frost. *_____

  Work 10-10-10 fertilizer into the soil at the rate of one cup for every 10 sq. ft. Plant the seedlings up to the lowest leaf because the stem under the first set of leaves will produce roots. Seedlings should be about 12 to 18 inches apart. You can interplant lettuce with broccoli—alternate the broccoli transplants with lettuce that you direct seeded earlier or with lettuce seedlings that you're putting in at the same time as the broccoli. Cover the plant with row cover, which is a thin cheese-cloth like material that lets in water and air. You can place it directly on the plants or drape it over wire or curved plastic pipe to protect the seedlings. Mulch to keep in the moisture.

For a fall crop, plant seed in July. Plant the seeds about ½ inch deep and about four inches apart. Use compost to lightly cover the seed. Thin the seedlings to 12 inches apart when they are about four inches tall and fertilize with about two tablespoons of high nitrogen fertilizer.

◆ *CARE*—When the seedlings are three weeks old, work two to three tablespoons of high nitrogen fertilizer into the soil around the side of each plant. This is called side dressing. Watch for pests and spray as needed.

◆ *HARVEST*—Seedlings planted in the early spring should be ready sometime in June and the fall crop can be harvested in September. Cut the main stem at a 45° angle a little below the head when the head is full and the buds are tight. Don't let the plant begin to turn yellow.

If you side dress the stem of the broccoli that's left after the first cutting with a couple of tablespoons of 10-10-10 fertilizer, you might encourage the plant to produce more heads.

CABBAGE

My mother's favorite childhood book was *Mrs. Wiggs of the Cabbage Patch* and my father's favorite meal was corned beef and cabbage, and as a result, cabbage was always a special vegetable in our house. Many cultures have traditional cabbage recipes and it can be cooked in a variety of ways, so it's a good staple for your garden. Cabbage is another crop that can be grown in both the spring and the fall.

◆ *PLANT*—Cabbage grows best in cool weather and it's recommended to put in seedlings instead of seeds so the plants are fully grown before the weather gets too hot. You can get the little plants into the ground as early as two weeks before the last frost. *_____. The recommended soil temperature is 45° to 75° and the ideal pH is about 6.8 to 7.0. Before you plant, add some compost or 1½ cups of 10-10-10 fertilizer into every 10 feet of soil. Cabbages should be planted about 18 to 24 inches apart, depending on the size of the mature cabbage. Plant the seedlings right down to the first set of leaves. Be prepared to protect the seedlings if the temperature has a sudden severe drop, but if you've hardened off your seedlings for a few days, they should be tough enough to withstand temperatures in the thirties.

If you plant seeds instead of seedlings, wait until the soil temperature is at least 50° and plant the seeds about ¼ to ½ inch deep and about five inches apart. When the sprouts come up, thin them to 18 to 24 inches apart. You can plant seeds in June if you want a fall crop of cabbage.

◆ *CARE*—When vegetables are "heavy feeders," it doesn't mean that they eat a lot and get fat, but it does mean that they need more fertilizer than most. Besides fertilizing the transplants when you put them into the ground, give them another shot when they're about a month old. Use 10-10-10 fertilizer and work two to three tablespoons into the soil around the side of each plant. Cabbages are attractive to insects, so do the usual checking of the leaves and spraying at the first sign of aphids or flea beetles. If you see cabbage worms strolling across your vegetables, you can either pick them up *(yuck!)* and throw them out or spray them with Bacillus thuringiensis, which is organic. Another thing you can do to protect the plants from bugs is cover them with a very light row cover.

◆ *HARVEST*—Your cabbages will be ready to harvest 55 to 80 days after you plant them. When you harvest your cabbages, cut them with a knife at the stem, and wrap them in any leaves that have fallen to the ground. If you planted seeds instead of seedlings in the spring, it will take the cabbages an extra month to mature. You can plant a fall crop in July, and the cabbage will be ready to harvest in September or October, or you can dig up the cabbage roots and plant kale instead for a little variety.

 Give vegetables from your garden as presents. You'll save money and also be giving the gift of health to your recipient.

CARROTS

Carrots are beautiful and delicious and good for your eyes, but don't plant them unless your garden has: 1) Very loose soil with no rocks or stones in it and 2) a gardener who enjoys thinning. Carrots are a root vegetable so they must be seeded directly—no transplants—and the soil must be loamy enough for the carrots to develop strong roots. It's difficult to grow carrots in clay soil and easier in sandy soil. Since the seeds are small and planted very close to each other, once they come up there's a lot of thinning to do. That said, if you still want to plant carrots, here's how.

♦ *PLANT*—Work extra compost into the soil to get it to a loamy consistency. The soil should be about 60°, so plant the carrot seeds right after your last frost date *_____. Plant the seeds every ¼ inch about ¼ inch deep and cover with germination mix or sifted compost. Water lightly. Some people mix radish and carrot seeds together before planting and put them in the ground all together. The radishes come up more than a month before the carrots, so there's plenty of room for both of them. Carrot seeds take about 21 days to germinate and the bed should be kept moist but not soaked that whole time. When the seedlings begin to come up, thin to about two inches apart.

♦ *CARE*—Keep the carrots moist as they grow. If you see the orange part of the carrot beginning to show through the soil, cover it. To avoid carrot fleas, cover the seedlings with row cover.

♦ *HARVEST*—Carrots should be ready to pull anywhere from 2 to 2½ months after planting. They should have a bright color and a crisp texture. Water deeply about two days before you harvest your crop, then just pull them up and enjoy them.

CHARD

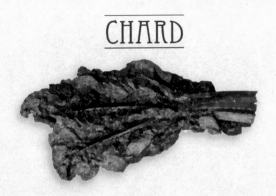

Chard is a great crop for your garden because it's packed with vitamins and minerals. It will grow in the cool weather and continue on into the heat of summer unlike many greens. You can plant chard early on its own, or you can put it in later where your spinach used to be. Chard is actually a member of the beet family and you can see the resemblance in the red ribs of some of the varieties.

- *PLANT*—Germinating chard seed for transplanting is not a good idea. You can plant seeds outside as early as three weeks before the last frost*_____ and continue to seed until three weeks after because the ideal soil temperature ranges from 50° to 75°. Loosen the soil and work in balanced fertilizer at the rate of one cup to every 10 square feet before planting. Plant the seeds about ½ inch deep every two to three inches, and when they're three or four inches tall, thin them to eight to 12 inches apart. Water lightly.

- *CARE*—Chard is relatively disease free, but still watch for bugs, and spray if you have to or cover the plants with row cover. When the plants are six inches high, side dress with one tablespoon of high nitrogen fertilizer to encourage leaf growth. Keep evenly moist.

- *HARVEST*—Although the exact time will vary according to when you planted it, your chard crop will be ready about two months after you put the seeds in the ground. You can either harvest the outside leaves and let the middle of the plant continue to grow or you can cut the whole plant down when it gets to be around one foot tall.

CHINESE CABBAGE

The garden plan in this book gives a choice between planting Chinese cabbage or endive. If you like Asian food, then choose the Chinese cabbage. When the leaves are fresh they are used like lettuce in salads and when they're cooked, they taste like cabbage. The Chinese cabbage family includes loose leaf varieties like Pac Choi and head varieties like Wong Bok.

- ◆ *PLANT*—Most people plant Chinese cabbage in the fall, but if you'd like to plant it in the spring, use seedlings to put in the soil to get a head start and avoid the warm weather. Work the soil and add compost to make it loamy, then add one cup of 10-10-10 fertilizer to every ten square feet of the row. Put the seedlings in the ground during the week after the last frost *_____ and place them about from 12 to 18 inches apart. Water lightly.

  You can plant seeds directly into the ground for a fall crop by preparing the ground according to the directions above and planting the seeds to a depth of ¼ to ½ inch and a distance of three inches. When the seedlings are four inches tall, thin them to 12 to 15 inches apart and side dress each with a teaspoon of 10-10-10 fertilizer.

- ◆ *CARE*—Check Chinese cabbage for insect pests and spray if necessary or else cover with a light row cover. Keep the plot moist but not soaking. Fertilize with one teaspoon of 10-10-10 fertilizer every three weeks after the plants have been thinned.

- ◆ *HARVEST*—For a spring crop, harvest the entire head as soon as it matures, otherwise it will bolt. If you're harvesting in the fall, you can cut off outer leaves of the plant when they reach 10 inches, or you can wait and cut the entire head.

CUCUMBERS

Cucumbers have been growing for over 10,000 years. Now that's an old vegetable! During those years farmers and breeders have made many improvements to this vegetable and now it's possible to get seeds that are specialized to grow in many different areas and appeal to a smorgasbord of tastes. Cucumbers come in two basic types, those for slicing and those for pickling, so make sure you know which kind you want before you buy your seeds.

◆ *PLANTING*—Cucumbers can't stand cold weather, so plant them two to three weeks after the last frost when the ground is above 65°. *_____. If you want to transplant cucumbers, you have to make absolutely sure that the seedling is not in a plastic pot because the transplanting will disturb the cuke's roots and it will suffer and probably die. If you buy or start your own seedlings in peat or paper pots, you can transplant the whole pot into the ground and all will be well. Before you plant the seed-lings, add a little extra compost or peat moss to the soil because cucumbers have shallow roots and the soil needs to be able to hold moisture. On the other hand, you don't want puddles on the top of the garden, so work the material in well so the soil drains eas-ily. While you're at it, add one to two tablespoons of balanced fertilizer to the soil around each plant. Plant seedlings three to four feet apart from each other. To save space in the garden, put them near a trellis so they can grow up instead of out. One or two cucumber plants usually provide enough of a crop for a family of four.

To plant seeds, prepare the soil with compost and fertilizer as described above and make a little hill for each place you want a plant to grow. Place your trellis by the hill and then plant four seeds about ½ inch deep evenly spaced around each hill. The hills should be three to four feet apart. Water lightly. When the seedlings begin to grow, thin to one or two plants per hill.

♦ **CARE**—Trim off any yellow leaves that you see as the vines grow, and do the usual pest patrol. Planting onions or tomatoes by your cucumbers will discourage pests. Mulch the plants after about three weeks. When the plants begin to blossom, side dress them by putting one to two tablespoons of balanced fertilizer a few inches from the stems of the plant. Don't overwater, but don't let the soil around the plants get dry, either.

♦ **HARVEST**—The cucumbers should start to reach maturity about two months after the seeds were planted. Pick them when they reach the length described on the seed packet. The cucumber should be firm and most of them, although not all, will have dark green skin. Pick them as they ripen and the vine should continue to produce for the rest of the season.

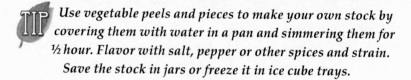

Use vegetable peels and pieces to make your own stock by covering them with water in a pan and simmering them for ½ hour. Flavor with salt, pepper or other spices and strain. Save the stock in jars or freeze it in ice cube trays.

EDAMAME

(Soy Beans)

Edamame, a great source of protein and vitamins, is becoming very popular in the U.S. The beans are boiled in the pod and shelled after cooking. They make an addicting snack.

- ◆ **PLANT**—Make sure the soil is over 65° when you plant edamame seeds. This would be about two weeks after the last frost.*_____. Beans like soil that is slightly acidic, in the 5.5 to 6.5 range, so you can adjust your soil accordingly. Plant the seeds about one inch deep and about four inches apart. Water. Edamame beans don't need any trellis support as they grow.

- ◆ **CARE**—Mulch around the beans and make sure the soil around them doesn't dry out. If you see any insects or fungus on the plants, spray them—or you can pick them off if they are beetles. No extra fertilization is necessary for the beans.

- ◆ **HARVEST**—Edamame will be ready for harvest about 2½ months after planting. They're ready when the pods look full and you can feel the beans touching each other. Don't let the pods yellow or the beans won't taste very good.

> *Add leftover dry cooked beans to make ground beef go further when you're making meatloaf or hamburgers. Mix cooked beans with chopped onions and grated cheese for a tasty and nourishing sandwich spread.*

ENDIVE

The garden plan in this book gives a choice between planting Chinese cabbage or endive. If you're into specialty greens, choose endive, which is grown as much for its beautiful looks as it is for its unique flavor. If you'd like a continuous crop of endive, seed new rows about every three weeks.

◆ **PLANT**—Endive likes a little warmer weather than most greens, so plant it out a week before the last frost. *_____.
Work the soil well and add compost to make it loamy, then add one cup of 10-10-10 fertilizer to every 10 square feet of the row. Plant the seeds from ¼ to ½ inch deep and cover with light soil. Water lightly.

◆ **CARE**—Water regularly and if you see pests, spray them.

◆ **HARVEST**—Endive should be ready to pick in about two months. Dig the plant from the ground and rinse it in cold water.

KALE

Kale to the chef! You can get this green to the chef in your family so he or she can add it to stir-fries or salads, or cook it with olive oil and garlic as a special treat.

- *PLANT*—Plant kale a week after the last frost,* _____ or even better, wait until you've harvested your cabbage and plant the kale in July for a fall crop. Kale favors soil that is slightly acid and loamy, so add a little compost and also about one cup of 10-10-10 fertilizer to every 10 square feet of soil. Plant the seeds ½ inch deep and four to six inches apart and cover with light compost or germination mix. Water lightly. Thin to 12 inches apart when the plants are four inches tall. If you're putting in transplants, prepare the soil as above and place them 12 inches apart.

- *CARE*—Kale is a hardy plant, but as always, keep your eyes open and spray at the first sign of insects. Side dress with one to two tablespoons of 10-10-10 fertilizer when the plants are eight inches tall.

- *HARVEST*—You can start to harvest the leaves when they're about ten inches. When you do this, cut off the outer leaves and leave the inner part so the plant can continue to grow. Don't worry about cold weather because light frost actually improves the flavor of kale.

LETTUCE

If you've never tasted home-grown lettuce, you've got a real treat in store. The lettuce from your garden will taste nothing like the lettuce from the grocery store, which usually tastes like nothing. There are five basic types of lettuce and they sound like the line-up for the program at an indie rock concert—crisphead, Romaine, loose leaf, butterhead, and buttercos. Each of the basic types has a bunch of varieties, so you have a huge choice of lettuce seeds. If you want to have fresh salads all season long you can do succession planting, choosing varieties that can withstand more heat for the summer seeding.

◆ **PLANT**—Lettuce is one of the coolest of cool weather crops and can be planted out in the garden up to five weeks before the last frost when the soil is only 40°. *_____. If you have a partially shady area of your garden, lettuce will love it there. Loosen the soil and work in one cup of 10-10-10 fertilizer for each 10 square feet of planting area, lay the seeds on top, cover with light compost or germination mix and pat down gently on top of the seeds. Water lightly. When the plants are about three inches tall, thin to 12 inches apart for loose leaf varieties and 14 inches apart for all other types.

If you're going to put in seedlings, follow the soil preparation above and plant the seedlings 12 or 14 inches apart depending on the variety.

◆ **CARE**—Lettuce is fairly easy to care for. The seedlings can withstand cold temperatures but if you have rain or snow, cover them with a flower pot, pail or yogurt or margarine container because you don't want the leaves to get wet and freeze. As the weather gets warmer, make sure to keep the plot watered. Fertilize head lettuce when the head begins to form which is about three weeks after transplanting or four weeks after seeding.

◆ *HARVEST*—The lettuce should be ready to harvest anywhere from one to two months after you plant the seeds, depending on what variety you chose. If you cut the leaves from the outside, the plant will keep growing. The leaves will be crisper if you harvest in the morning.

MUSTARD GREENS

If you like Asian food, mustard greens are a good choice for your garden. You can plant them early in the spring or late in the summer because they don't like warm weather. Follow the Chinese Cabbage planting directions.

ONIONS

Did you know that onions have biological time clocks? The many different varieties of onions are divided into two categories—long day and short day. Long day onions are better for the north because the longer day allows the onion to grow lots of green which in turn produces bigger bulbs. Short day onions have a different make up and need the southern day length to start their growing process. I don't know how long it took farmers to figure this out, but somehow they did and it's a good thing for us.

◆ *PLANTING*—The easiest way for gardeners to grow onions is to buy them as bulbs in what are called sets. If you'd like big onions, plant the sets indoors in February. For regular size onions, plant the bulbs directly into the ground. Keep the green top of the onion on the transplants trimmed to 3 in. before you plant it outside. Both the transplants and the bulbs go out about one week after your last frost date. *_____. Before you plant, work compost into the soil to loosen it and add one cup of 10-10-10-fertilizer for every 10 square feet of planting ground. Plant the bulbs with the pointy side up and put it deep enough to just cover the bulb. If you're putting transplants into the ground, plant them so the bulb is underground and the greens are above. Space both the bulbs and the transplants four inches apart.

◆ *CARE*—Keep the beds weeded and deal with insects if they fly in. When you side dress the onions, put one to 1½ teaspoons of 10-10-10 fertilizer around the side of each plant. Do this three times before you pick them: once three weeks after setting them out, once when the greens are six inches high, and once when the bulbs begin to swell. Keep onions well watered as the bulbs grow.

◆ *HARVEST*—If you planted scallions, pull them when they're six to eight inches tall. For the big onions, wait until a little less than half of the tops have fallen over. At this point the outer skin of the onion should be papery. Gently push over the rest of the tops, being careful not to break them. Wait a few more days and dig or pull up the onions. If you're going to store the onions, dry them in a warm place with good circulation before you put them away.

 If you live north of the Colorado/New Mexico border, plant long day onions. If you live south of this border, plant short day onions.

PEAS

Thomas Jefferson, an avid gardener, used to engage in a contest with his neighbors to see who could "bring the first pea to table." Being Thomas Jefferson, he usually won. Even today, getting peas to the table early is still a goal. Peas that you grow yourself taste sweet, almost like dessert. Pea Pie, anyone? You have your choice of three types of peas: shelling peas, which are self-explanatory; snap peas, which are similar to snap beans; and snow peas, which have much smaller peas than the other two and are grown for their pod as much as for their pea.

◆ *PLANT*—Peas can be planted as soon as the ground can be worked, which means as soon as you can get a shovel into the soil without hitting anything frozen. If your soil tends to be wet in the spring, you might want to grow peas in a raised bed rather than in the ground. Soak the seeds in lukewarm water for eight to 12 hours to soften the shell. You don't have to add compost to the soil, but it is helpful to dust the pea seeds *(which are actual peas)* with a special inoculant which protects the seed and increases the nitrogen-fixing nodules on the plant. This in turn encourages bigger plants and also helps the soil. You can get inoculant at garden stores and through seed catalogs. Follow the directions on the package.

Once the seeds are soaked and inoculated, make a one inch furrow and work in about a cup of 5-10-10 fertilizer for every 10 feet of your row. Put the peas in the furrow about one inch apart. Cover the furrow with soil and water lightly. If you're growing a climbing variety, have some sort of a trellis near the peas so you can start training them up the support as soon as they put out tendrils. Water lightly.

If you're planting seedlings, put them out up to five weeks before the last frost. Follow the directions for soil preparation and space them about two inches apart. If rain is in the forecast when the temperature is below freezing, cover the seedlings so they don't get soaked, but take the cover off as soon as the sun comes out.

◆ **CARE**—Do the usual watching for and spraying of insects. Mulch the roots of the peas and water regularly, but make sure not to get the vines too wet. As the peas grow, make sure vining types are growing up the trellis and not on the ground. Give the peas a little extra water when the pods begin to swell.

◆ **HARVEST**—Peas are ready to harvest when the pods are full but the shell is not very hard. This will usually be sometime in June from two to 2½ months after you first planted the seeds. Use your fingernails or a small scissor to snip the pea from the vine. You can also harvest the pea tendrils to use in oriental dishes or salads.

PEPPERS

Some like it hot, some like it sweet. However you like it, you can get what you want with peppers, a tasty, colorful vegetable that will be a treasured member of your garden.

◆ **PLANT**—All peppers need hot weather to grow, so it's best to plant seedlings rather than seeds so your plants are up and running once the weather warms up. Wait until the soil temperature is above 65° and the nighttime temperatures are over 50°. This should be three to four weeks after the last frost. *_____.

Dig a hole big enough to put the seedling all the way down to the bottom of the lowest leaf and work a teaspoon of balanced fertilizer into the soil in each hole. Plant the pepper and water lightly. Cover the soil with silver, black or red plastic mulch, which keeps the ground warm and helps the pepper grow. If your night temperatures are going to dip, cover the plants with row cover.

◆ *CARE*—Water regularly and deeply. Use a wire tomato cage *(see page 57)* around the pepper if the plant is beginning to tip over. If the weather gets really hot, consider putting a layer of organic mulch or newspaper under the plastic mulch. Spray at the first sign of insects. Every four weeks, side-dress with a tablespoon of 10-10-10 fertilizer.

◆ *HARVEST*—Peppers are usually ready to harvest in two to 2½ months after planting. Start picking them when they look ready to use and are the right color for their variety—yellow, green, red or orange. Be aware that all peppers, even the brightly colored ones, will start off as green. If you pick the peppers as they ripen, there's more of a chance for a bigger crop.

Save some money by adding leftover vegetables to a large container or plastic bag that you keep in your freezer. As the container fills up, use it to make soup or stew.

RADISHES

Speedy, helpful, flexible, unassuming, easy to get along with and attractive. This sounds like the description of an ideal employee, but in fact it's a list of the qualities of a radish. Radishes are one of the earliest crops to mature. They help keep insects away from cabbage, peas, lettuce and squash. They can be planted at any time throughout the season. Their small size makes it possible for them to fit anywhere in the garden. They can grow inter-planted with just about any other vegetable, and their gorgeous color and snappy taste make them a treat at the table. What more could you ask for?

◆ *PLANT*—Plant radish seeds three weeks to a month before the last frost. *_____. Loosen the soil to about three inches deep by working in compost and about a cup of balanced fertilizer for every 15 feet of the row. Plant the seeds about ½ inch deep and ½ to one inch apart and cover with germination mix. If you want to make life easy for both you and the radish, cover the seeds with a layer of row cover. Water lightly. You can mix carrot seeds and radish seeds and plant the all in the same row. The radishes will be up early and help to loosen the soil for the carrots. If you're inter-planting with other vegetables, plant the radishes in the row that you have planned for those vegetables. For a fall crop, plant the seeds in early August.

◆ **CARE**—Radishes have two growing requirements—water and room. Make sure to water evenly to a depth of three inches. Plant three inches apart so the roots have enough room. If you put row cover over the plants, insects should stay away.

◆ **HARVEST**—Radishes are usually ready to pick three weeks to a month after seeding and they should be picked right when they're ready in order to get the best texture and flavor. You'll know it's time to pick when they're bright and crunchy. Don't let them stay in the ground too long because an old radish is not a tasty radish. If you'd like, you can let a couple of radishes go to seed and harvest the seed pods to use in oriental cooking or for a snack.

SPINACH

Some vegetables are lucky enough to have festivals in their honor, and spinach is one of them. If you go to Crystal City, Texas during the second week of November, you can take part in the festivities, which include viewing the Popeye statue in front of city hall. If you can't make it, then grow your own spinach and have a festival at home.

◆ **PLANT**—Spinach is another cool weather crop, so you can plant seeds four to six weeks before the last spring frost and put seedlings in the ground a month before. *_____.
Work compost and high nitrogen fertilizer into the soil at the rate of one cup for every 10 square feet. Spinach doesn't grow well in acid soil, so if your soil tends toward acidity, add a little lime. Plant the seeds ½ inch deep and one inch apart and water lightly. Thin to four inches when the leaves begin to touch and make sure to eat the thinnings because they're delicious! Spinach seeds can be planted again in late August or September. If you're transplanting seedlings, put them in the prepared ground five to six weeks before the last frost and space them four inches apart.

◆ **CARE**—Keep spinach evenly watered and the area weeded. If any leaves start to have brown blotches, cut those leaves off and destroy them. The blotches are a sign of spinach leaf miners and sprays won't kill them, but removing the diseased leaves will keep the insects from spreading.

◆ **HARVEST**—Spinach will be mature about 1½ months after seeding. You can harvest the leaves as they become ready or cut the entire plant when it matures. If you leave the roots in the ground, you may get a few shoots later on.

SQUASH

Most of us have heard stories about gardeners sneaking around in the middle of the night to leave piles of zucchini on their neighbor's doorsteps because they themselves are zucchinied out. There's truth to these stories—summer squash is one of the most prolific producers of all the vegetables, so if you want to feel like a master gardener, plant squash. They're delicious, nutritious, and they just keep coming.

You'll find two basic types of squash in the seed catalogs—summer squash and winter squash. Summer squash matures in about 55 days and winter squash takes twice that long. Within the summer squash category, you can choose from zucchini, patty pan, green summer and yellow summer varieties . Winter squash has a choice of butternut, buttercup, acorn, delicata, hubbard and spaghetti.

◆ **PLANT**—Since squash likes warm weather, plant seeds or transplants one to two weeks after the last frost. *_____.
Work ½ gallon of compost and a cup of balanced fertilizer into the soil to a depth of at least six inches—12 is better. Lay some black plastic mulch over the planting area and cut an "X" in each spot you're going to plant a seedling. Pull back the triangle shapes to

open space to the soil. Make sure the space is big enough to allow water to get to the plant. If you're planting seeds, make a four to five inch mound of soil and place four seeds around the edge of the mound. Cover and water lightly. When the seeds sprout, thin to two plants. Space the mounds three feet apart for bush types and five or six feet apart for vining types. Squash takes up a lot of room, so you might want to plant the vining types at the edge of your garden and let them spread onto the surrounding non-garden area.

◆ *CARE*—Since you've enriched the soil and put down mulch before you planted, the main thing you'll have to do to take care of the squash is to keep it watered. If you should see bugs, pick them off or spray them. Once you have a few winter squash beginning to form, start pinching the flowers off the vine as they begin to form. This allows the plant energy to go to the squash instead of the flowers

◆ *HARVEST*—You can harvest summer squash at all stages of its growth, but it will be mature between 1½ and two months after seeding. Squash will continue to grow and get huge if you leave it on the vine, but you'll be sacrificing taste for size, so unless you want to use your squash as a weapon, pick right as it reaches maturity. Winter squash takes twice as long to mature as summer squash, so leave it on the vine until just after the first light frost. When you cut the squash from the vine or bush, leave one to two inches of stem on the vegetable.

When zucchini is at its height, our town has a zucchini race for the kids. The idea is to put wheels on a zucchini, decorate it, and the fastest and best-looking zucchini wins the prize. You might want to try this.

TOMATOES

Picture a vegetable garden in your mind. Chances are, tomatoes are the center of attention in your imaginary plot. Now you can bring your gardening daydream to life by planting your own delicious tomatoes. Before I get to the details, here is some tomato terminology for you. Determinate tomatoes grow on bushes and the fruits tend to mature within a week or two of each other. Indeterminate tomatoes grow on vines and once they start blooming, they'll continue to produce fruit until the first frost. Within these two categories are five types. Slicing tomatoes are large and round, ranging from a few ounces to two pounds. Paste tomatoes are usually plum shaped and used in sauces. Cherry, grape and currant tomatoes look like the fruit they're named after. Heirloom tomatoes are a type of slicing tomato that is grown from seed that has been passed down through the generations. Each type has many varieties, so you have plenty of choices when it comes to tomatoes.

♦ *PLANT*—Tomatoes do best if they're put in the ground as seedlings rather than seeds. The best time to do this is three to four weeks after the last frost. *_____. If your soil is acid, add a little lime or bone meal to neutralize it. Before you transplant, work compost and about ⅓ cup of 5-10-5 fertilizer into the soil where each plant will be set. After you've worked the soil, cover it with red plastic mulch and cut holes for the plants. Pinch off the bottom two leaves of the tomato and dig a hole deep enough to go right up to the bottom of the last leaf. The buried part of the stem will produce roots and make the plant stronger.

 Add some crushed eggshell to the bottom of the hole when you plant tomatoes to help prevent blossom rot.

Leave two feet between determinate varieties and 2½ feet for indeterminate. Put a tomato cage made of concrete reinforcement wire that's been shaped into a three to four foot high circle with a two foot diameter around each tomato plant. Water lightly.

◆ *CARE*—If the nights cool down after you plant your tomatoes, or if you want to plant them a week earlier than recommended, surround them with a Wall o' Water or similar protection. The Wall o' Water is a cone-shaped barrier made of plastic baffles to be put around the tomato plant. When the baffles are filled with water, they absorb the heat from the sun and release it at night, protecting your plants from the cold. You can get these at garden supply stores. You can also make a wrapper out of row cover or plastic and put it over and around tomato cages if you're using them. Water the tomatoes regularly and side-dress with a tablespoon of 5-10-5 fertilizer three times during the season: three weeks after transplanting, right before you pick your first tomatoes, and again two weeks later. Check for bugs and spray if necessary. Don't scream if you find tomato worms, which look like miniature dragons and actually rear up when you get near them. Use Bacillus thurengiensis instead.

◆ *HARVEST*—You'll know when to harvest your tomatoes—trust your instincts. Pick all remaining tomatoes right before the first frost even if they're still green. Once frost gets to them, they're gone.

TURNIPS

Did you know that turnips were used in Ireland as the original Jack-o'-lantern? Hollowing out a turnip and carving a face in it seems like too much work to me, but growing turnips to enjoy as the fall weather begins to turn cold is easy.

◆ **PLANT**—Although turnips can be planted in the spring, this garden plan suggests planting them in the fall as a succession crop to cabbage. The seeds can go in sometime in late August. Before planting, dig the soil and work in compost and two cups of balanced fertilizer to every 25 square feet of growing space. Plant seeds ½ inch deep and one inch apart and cover with light compost or germination mix. Water lightly. Thin to three inches apart when the greens come up. The young greens are very tasty, so be sure to try a bite.

◆ **CARE**—When the plants come up, mulch them and cover them with row cover, and you'll avoid insects. Water regularly and keep weeds out.

◆ **HARVEST**—You can harvest turnips after one month and they'll be small and very tender. If you want a bigger turnip, leave it in the ground for 40-50 days and then dig it up. Mashed turnips with butter, salt and pepper are very delicious.

GROW SOME HERBS

Humans have been cultivating and writing about herbs since Babylonian times, but Victory Gardens didn't include many herbs beyond chives and parsley. Today, though, herbs are "in" and considered important not only for enhancing the flavor of food, but also for their usefulness in remedies and cosmetics.

If you look at the garden plans on pages 2 and 3, you'll see that I've included a few annual herbs inter-planted with the vegetables in the garden. Because they're annuals, you can dig up their roots along with the vegetables at the end of the season. This plan is for a perennial herb garden, which stays in place from year to year.

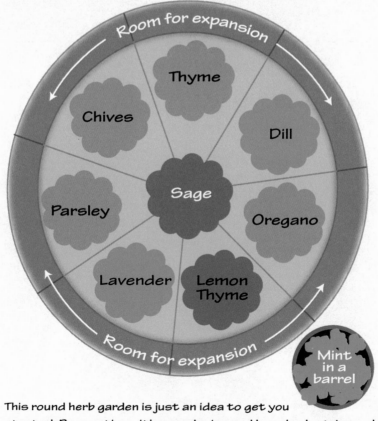

This round herb garden is just an idea to get you
started. Be creative with your design and keep herbs trimmed.

Since you'll be digging up and replanting the vegetable garden every season, it's not a good idea to have perennials scattered throughout the plot. Instead, I recommend that if you have space, you create your own perennial herb garden. Prepare the soil as you did for the vegetable garden. Herbs are some of the easiest plants to grow and the more you learn about them, the more you'll want to add to your garden. If you don't have room for the herbs in the ground, put them in pots. Let them stay on a patio, balcony, lawn or even a sidewalk during the summer, and carry them back inside to grow over the winter. Your life will be more complete if you have an herb or two around the house.

Here are Plant Profiles for a few herbs that you can use in cooking as well as in homemade remedies and cosmetics:

BASIL

According to *pokemyname.com*, one in every 4,131 Americans is named Basil. I bet you didn't know that. Considering all the wonderful qualities of this plant, I'm actually surprised that more people aren't named Basil.

◆ *PLANT*—You're better off planting basil seedlings rather than seeds. Plant the seedlings in enriched soil in sun to partial sun, 12 to 18 inches apart, one to two weeks after the last frost *_____. Basil is a good crop to interplant because it improves the flavor of almost all vegetables—even while it's growing! Experiment with many of the different varieties of basil. Basil is an annual and must be replanted every year.

◆ *CARE*—Don't over-water seedlings, but once the plants get to be about four inches, water regularly and make sure that the basil is protected if you have a period of scorching sun. Feed once during the growing season with a high nitrogen fertilizer.

◆ *HARVEST*—Cut basil leaves starting near the bottom of the plant from places where you see new leaves about to grow. Cut off flowers when they start to grow and use in pesto. When the plant seems to be "done", cut it all the way down to about one inch above the soil—sometimes you'll get a second growth, which is a wonderful surprise. Soak one cup of basil leaves in four cups of wine for an uplifting drink. Add basil flowers to your bath to relax.

CALENDULA

During the Civil War, doctors used calendula flowers to treat open wounds. Today the flowers are still used in healing ointments to treat bruises and sores.

◆ *PLANT*—Plant calendula in full sun right after the last frost. *_____. This is an annual that prefers semi-light soil, but will do well almost anywhere. Plant seeds three inches apart and thin to six to eight inches when the plants are two inches tall.

◆ *CARE*—Water regularly but don't let the soil get waterlogged. Pick flowers as they open to keep the plant blooming continuously.

◆ *HARVEST*—Pick the flowers when they are fully open if you plan to use them in recipes or as cut flowers. Fresh calendula petals can be sprinkled in salads and stews. The petals can also be used to give a tangy flavor to rice , cheese, yogurt or omelets.

CHIVES

We can thank Marco Polo for taking chives from China and introducing them to the rest of the world. Thank you, Marco.

◆ *PLANT*—Chives like a sunny location, although they tolerate partial shade. They'll grow in almost any conditions, but will produce more in rich well-drained soil. This perennial grows to about ten inches high.

◆ *CARE*—Chives develop round mauve flowers in midsummer. Water in dry spells and remove flowers for better flavor.

◆ *HARVEST*—When harvesting, leave 2" for growth next year.

Chives are used to flavor many dishes, and the flowers are used to decorate salads. They can be stored in a sealed plastic bag for seven days, frozen in ice cubes, or dried. The plant deters aphids.

CILANTRO / CORIANDER

It's said that people have a genetic pre-disposition to either love or hate cilantro. If you're one of the folks who doesn't like cilantro, leave the plant into the ground until it goes to seed, and you'll wind up with coriander which was used in love potions in the Middle Ages. Not often do you find an herb with such a split personality.

◆ *PLANT*—Plant cilantro in full sun to part shade about two inches apart a couple of days after the last frost. *_____
Since it's an annual, it will go to seed sometime during the middle to late summer. The seeds of cilantro are known as coriander and have a sweet, spicy scent and flavor and can be harvested as soon as the pod begins to open.

◆ *CARE*—Water when dry.

◆ *HARVEST*—The plant grows to about 10 inches and can be harvested anytime until it reaches full growth. Cilantro is used in Mexican, Indian, Thai and Chinese foods. The leaves can be frozen or put in water to keep fresh. The stems can spice up soups and stews. The seeds can be used in tea or to flavor pies and cakes.

DILL

What's your favorite coin, nickels or dimes? This is the question my niece asks of people who are having a spell of hiccups. *(Try it sometime.)* Another way to stop those hiccups is to chew on a few dill seeds. How about that!

◆ *PLANT*—Dill will do best in soil that's been enriched with compost in a sunny plot that's protected from the wind. Try to plant dill at the edge of your garden because it has a bad effect on some other herbs and vegetables, especially fennel. Put the seeds about nine inches apart one week after the last frost. *_____

◆ *CARE*—Water regularly.

◆ *HARVEST*—Pick the dill leaves when they're still young, and cut the stem and seed heads just after flowering when the seeds begin to form.

To collect dill seeds easily, turn the stem and seed head upside down in a paper bag, put a rubber band around the top of the bag and hang in a cool dry place. The seeds will fall into the bag and be ready for you to use.

LAVENDER

I believe that it's impossible to say too many good things about lavender. This is the scent of peace. If you're having a bad day, spend some time sniffing lavender, and you'll feel much better.

- ◆ *PLANT*—Lavender is an perennial that is better planted as a seedling. I know a few people who have grown lavender from seed—but only a few. Put your seedlings 18-24 inches apart right around the date of the last frost. *_____ If you're planting outdoors, loosen the soil and add lime, if necessary, to get it to an alkaline level. Make sure to buy a variety that will grow well in your part of the country. Lavender is a perennial in zones 5 through 9, but if you can't grow it outside, try it as an indoor plant.

- ◆ *CARE*—Lavender likes dry conditions, so water, but don't over-do it.

- ◆ *HARVEST*—Lavender leaves can be harvested at any time, and lavender flowers can be cut once the flowers are fully opened. Different types of lavender mature at different times, so watch your lavender carefully. To dry lavender, bundle a few stems, wrap with a rubber band and hang upside down in a well-ventilated dark room.

MINT

If mint didn't taste so good it would be considered a weed because it grows like crazy. For those who doubt their gardening ability, plant mint. It won't disappoint.

◆ *PLANT*—Once you have mint in your garden, you have it all over your garden, and since it's a perennial it doesn't go away. For this reason, make sure you use a container for your mint plants instead of putting into the ground. Half whiskey barrels are especially good for growing mint. Fill the barrel with potting soil enriched with a balanced fertilizer and a little lime. Plant seedlings 12 inches apart one week after the last frost. *_____. If you want to grow mint indoors, put one plant in a 12 inch pot.

◆ *CARE*—Once mint is growing, it doesn't need much care—just water it when it gets dry.

◆ *HARVEST*—Pick the leaves at any time during growth. As with oregano, picking encourages growth.

OREGANO

If you want bees and butterflies in your garden, plant oregano. This perennial is an easy-care mainstay in all herb gardens.

◆ *PLANT*—Oregano likes to be planted in a sunny spot that gets shade in the afternoon. The soil should be well-drained, enriched and alkaline. Plant seedlings rather than seeds to

get the best growth. Put plants in two weeks before the last frost
*_____ 12 to 18 inches apart.

◆ **CARE**—Water on a regular basis and cut the plants down to about
three inches from the ground before the last frost.

◆ **HARVEST**—Pick oregano leaves at any time. Cutting actually
stimulates growth.

PARSLEY

Wearing a wreath of parsley is said to prevent drunkenness, so
you might want to wear it on your head to your next party and
see what happens.

◆ **PLANT**—Parsley, a biennial, should be planted in a sunny, sheltered area in well-drained soil up to three weeks before the last
frost. *_____ It can be grown indoors, but doesn't
do well when transplanted. If you germinate the seed early, make
sure to use a paper or peat pot so the roots aren't disturbed when
you transplant. If you plant the seeds directly, put four or five
seeds every 12 inches and either thin them when they're about
three inches high, or let them grow in a clump.

◆ **CARE**—Water regularly and spray if you see whiteflies.

◆ **HARVEST**—Italian parsley can grow to be two feet tall. Harvest the
lower leaves throughout the season. The herb can be used to flavor
cream cheese, pickles and curries. It is used as a garnish on many
dishes, and the leaves freshen breath when chewed. Parsley tea helps
to cure coughs and can be used to soothe babies with colic.

SAGE

If you want whiter teeth, rub them with sage leaves and if you have indigestion, try a sage leaf sandwich after meals. And you thought sage was just for turkey stuffing!

◆ **PLANT**—Plant sage in full sun in semi-light soil up to 4 weeks before the last frost. *_____ If you're planting seedlings, place them about 10 to 12 inches apart. If you're direct seeding, leave about three inches between the plants and thin them to 10 to 12 inches apart when they're about four inches high. Use the thinnings in cooking or hang them upside down and dry them. Sage grows to be from one to two feet high and produces little blue flowers, which are edible.

◆ **CARE**—Sage is a hardy perennial and will grow in many conditions, but it is best to keep it fairly dry if possible. If it's planted outside, cut back after flowering and prune frequently to keep bushy. If it's planted in a pot, keep it in a sunny location.

◆ **HARVEST**—Pick the leaves just before flowering for cooking or herbal preparations. Fresh sage leaves can be added to salad, and dried sage is used in many recipes, especially with poultry. To get the best flavor from dried leaves, dry them slowly in a cool, dark place.

THYME

Try putting a little thyme under your pillow if you want a good night's sleep. According to some, it might even help your psychic powers as you dream.

- ◆ **PLANT**—Plant thyme in full sun in well-worked soil. English thyme is a hardy perennial and will grow in many conditions, but it is best to keep it fairly dry if possible. The plant gets little mauve flowers and spreads by creeping, but it doesn't take over your garden.

- ◆ **CARE**—If you planted outside, prune frequently to encourage new growth. If planted in a pot, keep in a sunny location.

- ◆ **HARVEST**—Pick leaves when thyme is in bloom for best flavor. Thyme is used in meat and poultry dishes, and dried thyme leaves can be used to flavor oil and vinegar.

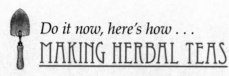

Do it now, here's how . . .
MAKING HERBAL TEAS

Steep one teaspoon of dried herbs or three teaspoons of fresh herbs in one cup of boiling water for five to 10 minutes. The longer you steep the herb, the stronger it will be. Strain and drink. Use the strained herbs to feed your houseplants and save money on plant food.

- **Basil tea** is good for respiratory ailments. It also detoxifies the liver. Use the leaves to make the tea.

- **Calendula tea** is helpful in relieving upset stomachs and menstrual cramps. Use the flowers to make the tea.

- **Coriander tea** is used to aid digestion and as a mild sedative. Use the seeds to make the tea.

- **Lavender tea** wards off depression and helps with sleep. Use both leaves and flowers to make the tea.

- **Mint tea** aids digestion and calms upset stomachs. Use the leaves to make the tea.

- **Oregano tea** helps reduce fevers, alleviate cold symptoms, avoid seasickness and relieve menstrual pain. Use the leaves and flowers to make the tea.

- **Parsley tea** helps detoxify the kidneys. Use the leaves to make tea.

- **Sage tea** is used to relieve sore throats and coughs, and aids digestion. When gargled, sage tea helps get rid of gingivitis and inflamed gums. Use the leaves and flowers to make the tea.

- **Thyme tea** is helpful for digestion problems. Use the leaves to make the tea.

SOME HERBAL PREPARATIONS MAY BE HARMFUL
DURING PREGNANCY. CHECK WITH YOUR DOCTOR
BEFORE USING ANY HERBAL TEAS OR OILS.

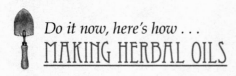

Do it now, here's how . . .
MAKING HERBAL OILS

The recipes listed here are for body and massage oils, not essential oils. Making essential oils requires pounds of fresh herbs that are then distilled. Making the body oils is much easier!

Heat almond, grapeseed or sesame oil to around 100 degrees. Drop in one leaf of the herb you're using to make sure it doesn't burn. When the oil is still very warm, but not hot enough to burn the leaves, add ½ cup of fresh herbs *(leaves, flowers and seeds)* to 1½ cups of oil. Steep the herbs in the oil for six to eight hours. Strain and add essential oil, which you can get at health food stores, to get the scent to where you like it. Pour into dark-colored bottles and store in a cool, dark place.

◆ *Basil oil* rubbed on the temples, head and neck relieves mental tension.

◆ *Calendula oil* soothes inflammations, cracked, chapped skin and lips. Reduces varicose veins and bruises.

◆ *Coriander oil* helps alleviate rheumatism.

◆ *Dill oil* strengthens nails.

◆ *Lavender oil* helps get rid of wrinkles and dry skin; heals burns and scrapes; relieves headaches when applied to temples.

◆ *Mint oil* relaxes sore muscles; great for massage.

◆ *Oregano oil* relieves toothache pain when rubbed on the gums; reduces swelling and arthritis pain. Use as a nasal wash to combat colds and flu.

◆ *Parsley oil* helps alleviate pain of sprains and bruises; stops itching of insect bites.

◆ *Sage oil* relieves pain when rubbed on rheumatic joints.

◆ *Thyme oil* facilitates healing of cuts and sores.

Once you start using herbs to make teas, oils and other products, it's hard to stop. Soon you'll be making gifts for everyone in your family and probably the mail deliverer and the garbage man, too. The following resources will open the doors of herbal knowledge for you:

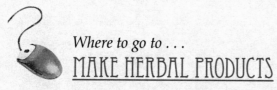

Where to go to . . .
MAKE HERBAL PRODUCTS

www.snowdriftfarm.com—A great collection of recipes *(formulary)* and products to help you make them.

www.oilsbynature.com—A good source for basic body oils.

The Herbal Body Book, Jeanne Rose, Perigree Books, ISBN 0-399-50790
  Good recipes and resources.

The Herbal Arts, Patricia Telesco, Citadel Press, ISBN 0-8065-1964-9
  Herb profiles and many recipes.

Making Plant Medicine, Richo Cech, Horizon Herbs, ISBN 0-9700312-0-3
  Very detailed directions.

Encyclopedia of Magical Herbs, Scott Cunningham, Llewellyn Publications,
  ISBN 0-87542-122-9—An alternative view of herbs and their uses.

CARE FOR YOUR GARDEN

Getting your plants into the ground is similar to sending your children off to kindergarten—you've raised them from tiny beings and now you've launched them out into the world. Well, this might be a stretch of a simile, but you do need to watch over your seedlings once they're planted. The five basic chores of any gardener throughout the growing season are fertilize, mulch, water, weed and protect. The final task we list is keeping track in a notebook of what's happening in the garden. This is something that doesn't have to be done, but it's a very big help if you do.

ᔥ *Fertilize* ᔥ

Do you want to know a fertilizer joke? A farmer was driving along the road with a load of fertilizer. A little boy, playing in front of his house, saw him and called, "What've you got in your truck?" "Fertilizer," the farmer replied. "What are you going to do with it?" asked the little boy.

"Put it on strawberries," answered the farmer.

"You ought to live here," the little boy advised him. "We put sugar and cream on ours."

People can laugh about fertilizer, but it's a serious matter. Unless you've been enriching your soil with compost and other organic material for years, you'll probably need to fertilize your garden for the best crop. When you're fertilizing, you're actually feeding the plants, usually through the roots, but sometimes through the leaves. The first time you go to buy fertilizer, you may feel like you need a decoder ring to figure out the numbers and letters on the packages, but it's really not that complicated. The three numbers on the bag stand for NPK, which in turn stand for nitrogen, phosphorus and potassium. These three elements are important for plant growth and are the mainstays of all fertilizers. The numbers indicate what percentage of each of the elements is in that particular fertilizer. A fertilizer that is labeled 5-10-5 has five percent nitrogen, 10 percent phosphorus and five percent potassium. This is a combination that might be used on younger plants which are in the process of developing a root system. A balanced fertilizer contains an equal percentage of NPK and a label for this fertilizer might be 10-10-10. A 10-10-10 balance is a good choice for an all-purpose fertilizer. Basically, the nitrogen encourages leaf growth, phosphorus helps stimulate the roots, and potassium builds up disease resistance and aids in development of fruits and flowers.

One other thing that you'll notice as you peruse the fertilizer aisles is that there are both liquid and granular forms. The liquid gets mixed with water and is sprayed on the soil and, sometimes, the leaves of the plants, and the granular is dug in around the stem of each plant. The liquid goes to work faster in your garden, but is also more likely to be washed away. The granular takes a little longer to work, but will remain in the soil longer. Granular fertilizer is what most gardeners use, but it's up to you to decide which you like best.

If you want to delve more deeply into the wonderful world of fertilizers, you'll find that there are many specialized varieties—for roses, vegetables, trees, lawns, perennials, houseplants, and more. Each of these has a different percentage for each of the three major elements. These specialized fertilizers makes it possible for you to custom-feed your plants.

More is not better in the case of fertilizers. Plants need to be nourished, but if you give them either too much fertilizer or too strong of a concentrate—the bag will have high NPK numbers—the leaves and roots will burn and the plant will suffer and possibly die. This is especially true of very young plants. You don't want to be known as a plant killer, so if you're not sure about what to do, go with less rather than more. Check the Plant Profiles to see how much and what type of fertilizer each of the vegetables in your garden will need, and work the fertilizer into the soil right before you begin to plant. Some plants won't need to be fertilized again and others require feeding two to four times a season.

ᛉ *Mulch* ᛉ

The next thing you do is mulch. The word "mulch" always sounded to me like a noise a cartoon animal might make, but in fact, it's a covering for the soil in your garden that keeps moisture and nutrients in and weeds out. Organic mulches include straw, hay, chopped alfalfa, grass clippings, newspaper, sawdust mixed with dried leaves, dried leaves without the sawdust, or compost. Spread the mulch over your soil to a depth of two to three inches. Since these mulches are organic, they will be absorbed into the soil over time, so they need to be replenished during the growing season. You'll know it's time to add more when you see the soil peeking through. You can buy these mulches in garden or farm stores, or gather them in your backyard.

Plastic is a non-organic mulch, and many plastic mulches are available in garden stores and catalogs. In the olden days, only black plastic was available, but now you can buy red and silver mulches as well. The red plastic helps tomatoes and the silver mulch is said to be good for hot weather crops such as peppers, eggplants and tomatoes because of its reflective qualities. If you decide to go with plastic mulch, lay it over the soil before you plant, cut X's in the plastic for each seedling, tuck the loose pieces under and leave a little space around each plant so fertilizer and water can get to the roots. Unless you have vicious wild animals in your garden, the plastic mulch should last for the whole season.

℘ *Water* ℀

Vegetables consist of 70 to 92% water, so watering is a very important part of your gardening regimen. Plants get most of their water through their roots, and the point of watering a garden is to get the moisture into the ground instead just wetting the surface. For a vegetable garden, a drip system usually works more effectively than a sprinkler because the water goes directly into the soil. You can have a watering system professionally installed, you can use soaker hoses, or you can make your own drip system with kits you can get at garden stores or in catalogs. A good site is *www.dripworks.com*. If you'd like to set up a system without buying a kit, here are some web sites to check out:

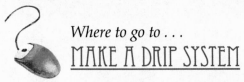

Where to go to . . .
MAKE A DRIP SYSTEM

www.diynetwork.com/diy/sw_watering_irrigation/
   Has complete directions online.

www.taunton.com/finegardening/pages/g00005.asp
   Links and clear directions for drip systems.

If you don't like drips and if you have sprinklers that you want to continue to use, try to set them so they water low, and if you're watering by hand, aim the head of the hose at the soil rather than the tops of the plants.

Punch holes in empty liter plastic bottles, cut off the bottoms, remove the caps and place upside down in your garden. Leave about two inches of the bottle above the soil and fill it every time you water. This is a slow-release method of watering plant roots.

There's nothing like a well-developed root system as far as vegetables are concerned, and the way to achieve this is to water deeply so the roots go far down in the earth to get the moisture. Rather than watering a little every day, which will let the roots get lazy because they'll stay near the surface where the water is, water less often but more deeply. Here's an obvious point—if you live in a humid climate, you'll be watering less than if you live in a dry climate. Watering two or three times a week for about twenty minutes each time should give your plants plenty of moisture no matter where you live. Just to be sure, try this watering schedule and then take a ruler and measure how many inches deep the water went. If it's between one to two inches, you're set.

Adjust your watering schedule to the weather, and if it's rained for a couple of days straight, you can skip the watering that week. If you water in the middle of the day, much of the water evaporates and never gets to the plants. If you water late in the evening, the leaves get wet and wet leaves at night invite disease. Work with nature and water in the morning so the plants have the day to absorb the water and dry out before the night comes.

One final word on watering—don't overdo it. If the leaves of your plants start turning yellow and the water starts puddling on the soil, you're watering too much.

❧ *Weed* ❧

In a way, I feel sorry for weeds because basically they're just decent plants growing in the wrong place. Although many weeds such as dandelions, nettles and shepherd's purse are actually beneficial to humans, they are still unwelcome when they show up in the vegetable garden because they take nutrients from the plants you're trying to grow. Besides that, they just look messy. Maybe some day someone will promote weed gardens in the name of plant equality, but in the meantime here are some ways to eliminate weeds in your garden.

The easiest way to keep weeds from growing is to have a fairly thick layer of mulch on the ground *(see pages 73-74)*. The mulch suffocates the weeds, and even if a few pop up through the mulch, their root systems are usually weak enough that you can easily pull them out. If you do see weeds growing, the best thing is to dig them up by their roots so they don't re-grow. You can also hoe them up. If you just pull at them and get the leaf portion off but leave the roots, you're in trouble, because the likelihood is that the roots remaining in the soil will send up more shoots. So the moral of the weeding story is to take the time to get the roots out of the soil, either by hoeing or digging. Once the weeds are up and out, throw them away—far away—from the garden.

In truth, weeding can become one of the more rewarding activities of your life because there's such a difference between the "before" and "after" garden. In fact, if you want to make yourself feel good, take a picture before you start weeding and another one after you're finished and congratulate yourself on a job well done.

Stay away from chemical weed killers because if they'll kill weeds, they'll kill the plants you want to keep, too. Even vinegar, which is totally organic and does a great job at killing weeds in places where there aren't other plants growing, will wipe out your garden. Weeding by hand is the way to go.

❧ *Eliminate* ☙

After spending time on planning and planting your garden, you will have no tolerance for pests that want to share your bounty. The best way to get rid of insect pests in your garden is not to have them in the first place, and the best way to do that is to have healthy plants. Insects are just not interested in a plant that is doing well, just as germs seem to ignore people with strong immune systems. If you give your vegetables rich soil, the right amount of water, and extra nutrients when they need them, the plants should thrive and be insect free. And you won't have to use the pesticides that we talked about in the Care sections of the Plant Profiles. But just in case some harmful insects make their way into your garden, here are some ideas for getting rid of them.

You'll find many pesticides both in garden stores and catalogs, but stay away from the formulas that are chemical-based because what goes on the plant, goes in the plant, and you'll wind up having traces of pesticide for dinner.

You can buy organic, meaning non-chemical, fertilizers in garden stores and order them from seed catalogs. Most organic pesticides are plant-based and non-toxic to humans. Neem is effective against whiteflies, aphids, spider mites and thrips and Ryania works on worms and borers. Both are good choices, but be aware that they must be applied directly to the insect and may have to be sprayed on for a couple of days before the bug dies. Pyrethrin is made from a species of daisy, and Sabadilla comes from the Sabadilla lily which grows in South America. Both of these are effective against most bugs, but they are both toxic to bees, so it's important to apply them when no bees are in the area, usually early morning or late evening. Bacillus thuringiensis *(Bt)* is good if you want to get rid of harmful worms and chewing insects. Insecticidal soap will work if you get to the pests before they multiply, and the soap is very helpful when mixed in some of the recipes below. Test all pesticides on a couple of leaves first because they may cause the leaves of some plants to burn and turn brown.

An excellent source for buying organic pesticides and fertilizers is *www.gardensalive.com*

Some general hints about using organic formulas:
 ◆ *Always spray and/or dust with pesticides in the early morning or late evening.*
 ◆ *Remember to spray both the top and the underside of the leaves.*
 ◆ *Treat just the infected plants, not the whole garden.*

One way you can protect plants from harmful insects is to drape them with floating row cover *(see page 35)*. Water and air get through to the plant, but most insects don't. The cloth and accessories are available in garden centers and from the seed catalogs on pages 6 and 7.

Do it now, here's how . . .
MAKE A PORTABLE PLANT PROTECTOR

Buy enough four to six inch mesh concrete reinforcement wire to make a tunnel big enough to place over your vegetables. This will probably be two to three feet wide, two to three feet high and three to four feet long. The size will vary with the plants you want to cover. Form the wire tunnel and drape it with row cover which you can attach with clip clothespins or staples. Anchor the protector with stakes or ground staples. You can also use light pvc pipes or heavy pieces of metal to make the tunnel. Make as many tunnels as you think you'll need to cover your plants if you start to see insects using your garden for a restaurant. As an extra bonus, you can also use these in case of an early snow or an surprise cold snap. Materials for one plant protector that is 18" high x 18" wide x 36" long should run about $7.00.

> *Lady bugs are a beneficial insect that help keep the smaller pests out of your garden. You can buy these through some seed catalogs and set them free in your garden.*

Even if you use lady bugs and row cover, still keep a close eye on the garden, just in case one of your plants should be attacked by bugs or fungus. At the first sign of trouble, take action. If the diseased plant is pretty far gone, dig it out and throw it away before the bugs start moving in on the rest of the garden. If you're vigilant, you'll catch the critters before they get settled in and you can treat them with the appropriate spray.

If you want to make your own pesticides, here are some recipes:

Do it now, here's how . . .
MAKE ORGANIC PESTICIDE

Pest	Recipe
Flea beetles, aphids, mealybugs, spider mites, thrips, and whiteflies	*Mix one cup of vegetable oil with one teaspoon of mild liquid dish washing or insecticidal soap. Shake well or mix with a stick blender, then add a quart of water. Spray.*
	OR—Mince one and a half bulbs of garlic and soak in three teaspoons of mineral oil for 24 hours. Strain into two cups of water, add one teaspoon of mild liquid dish washing soap and shake vigorously. Spray.

Chewing and sucking insects, aphids	Puree two small onions and two cloves of garlic. Add a chopped jalapeno pepper or one tablespoon of cayenne pepper. Soak in one gallon of water overnight. Strain. Extra can be refrigerated for two to three weeks.
Slugs	Put flat beer into a plate and the slugs will become drunk and drown. Pick the slugs up (this is more fun for kids than it is for adults) and throw them out or pour salt on them.

Have a grapefruit for breakfast and put the empty halves into the garden in the evening. The slugs will climb in because they like the scent and they won't be able to climb out.

Fungus	Mix one tablespoon of mild liquid dish washing detergent or insecticidal soap with one teaspoon of baking soda and one quart of water. Mix well.
Blackspot, powdery mildew, brown spot & other funguses	Mix one tablespoon of canola oil with four teaspoons of baking soda or potassium bicarbonate. Pour into one gallon of water and shake vigorously. Spray the plant but do not pour onto the soil.
Leaf Spot	Puree two cups of tomato leaves and mix with two tablespoons of cornstarch in 10 cups of water. Strain.

Some gardeners have a problem keeping larger animals out of their gardens. A two or three foot wire fence will work for rabbits and some dogs. Plastic owls and snakes keep some small animals away. Hot pepper, either jalapeno or cayenne, is a good deterrent for cats, dogs and squirrels. Deer are more of a problem because they can jump most fences. There are a few deer repellents on the market that sometimes work and I've also heard of people *(mostly men)* who have urinated around their gardens to keep the deer away. A barking dog works to deter all but the most brazen deer. The other option is to love the deer and feel good that you're making them happy every time they eat your plants.

Some recipes to keep the non-deer out of your garden:

Do it now, here's how . . .

MAKE ANIMAL REPELLENTS

Pest	Recipe
Gophers	Puree three garlic bulbs, eight jalapeno peppers, and three cups of water. Pour some of the mixture into each of the gopher holes. Put the end of a garden hose into the hole and turn the water on high.
Voles and Mice	Put a layer of wire mesh underneath the soil of your garden before you begin to cultivate.
Squirrels	Mix one tablespoon of Tabasco sauce, two tablespoons of cayenne pepper or chili powder and one teaspoon of liquid dish washing soap in a gallon of water. Spray around the plants.
	For container plants, wet cotton balls with a little cooking oil and then dip the cotton into cayenne pepper. Put the coated cotton balls in the container.
Cats and dogs	Puree one onion and three cloves of garlic, add to one quart of water and add one tablespoon of Tabasco sauce. Soak overnight, strain and spray around the garden. (Not on the plants.)

✂ *Protect* ✃

When the weather surprises you with unexpected cold, heat or rain, it's important to know how to protect your plants from the elements. A cloche is a glass or plastic bell-shaped device that's made especially for protecting plants in situations like these. You can order or buy them from many garden supply stores. If there's a cold snap, a heavy snow or a freezing rain, cover the plants with the cloche, upside-down flowerpots, cardboard boxes, yogurt or margarine containers or any other box-type container you can find. Necessity is the mother of invention, and you'll be surprised at what you can come up with when it comes time to protect your plants. We had a snowstorm in the middle of May one year, so we put blanket-draped card tables over the plants. It worked and the plants lived to see another day. Make sure you remove the covering when the sun comes back out and the weather warms up, otherwise your plants will get overheated, which is not good for them either.

Speaking of heat, when it's a very hot day you can expect to see the leaves of the plants wilt. This is their way of protecting themselves and they perk back up in the evening. If you have a protracted hot spell, though, it's a good idea to lightly spray the leaves with water daily and definitely check to make sure the ground doesn't dry out. Row covers can also be used to protect the plants from excessive cold or heat. The portable plant protector described on page 78 can be used to keep your plants warm as well as protect them from bugs.

℘ *Track* ℃

"Mary, Mary quite contrary, How does your garden grow?" was the nursery rhyme that my friends and I sang while we walked to elementary school. Keeping notes on how your garden grows is an important and usually pleasant part of being a gardener. There will be times that you feel contrary and don't want to write down what's going on, but try to keep up because you'll be glad that you kept track of your garden when Spring comes and it's time to plant again. The account that you keep will help you use your successes and failures of the past to point the way to an ever improving garden.

TYPES OF INFORMATION THAT'LL BE HELPFUL TO YOU:

- ◆ *The name of each vegetable*
- ◆ *Where you bought it*

- ◆ *The variety*
- ◆ *When you planted the plant or seeds*

- ◆ *When it matured*
- ◆ *Any problems?* (disease or pests)

- ◆ *How much it produced*
- ◆ *Any anecdotal information about growing habit*

- ◆ *Your opinion of the quality*

You might also want to note:

- ◆ *What pesticides you used*
- ◆ *Which fertilizers you used*

- ◆ *How effective they were*
- ◆ *How well they worked*

It's also a good idea to write down where you planted each vegetable so you know where to rotate (see page 89) the crops each year. And it doesn't hurt to write down how your garden makes you feel.

PRESERVING YOUR CROP

Eating vegetables fresh from the garden is an indescribable treat, but having your own tomatoes and beans for dinner in January is even better. Part of the goal of the original Victory Gardens was to produce food that the family could preserve for winter use. If you look at the vegetables in the garden, you'll notice that nearly all them can be preserved in one way or another. Giving you detailed directions on food preservation is beyond the focus of this book, but to get you started on your preservation venture, here's a summary of the different methods and a short source list that will lead you to everything you need to know to become an expert. The four basic ways to preserve food are canning, pickling, freezing, and drying. Different vegetables lend themselves to different methods.

Canning is not putting food into a can and covering it with aluminum foil, which is what I thought in my City Girl days. When you can vegetables, you put them in glass jars, cook them at a very high temperature, and hermetically seal them. Vegetables need to be heated in a canning pressure cooker, NOT a hot bath canner. The jars, seals and special canning equipment are available at many hardware stores, and even seed catalogs offer the equipment and directions for canning.

Beans, cabbage, beets, carrots, peas, tomatoes, peppers and squash can all be canned.

Pickling involves making a brine solution of pickling salt, water and other spices and soaking the vegetables in the brine for a period of time.

Chinese cabbage, peppers, carrots, cucumbers, onions, and green beans are candidates for pickling.

Freezing vegetables from your garden is easy: cook them in boiling water for a couple of minutes—this is called blanching—and then place them in moisture proof containers before you put them in the freezer.

Beans, kale, mustard greens, peas, chard, spinach and winter squash freeze well.

Drying vegetables is as simple as putting them on a drying rack made of window screen stretched over a wooden frame. You can also cook them at a very low heat in your oven, or use a dehydrator which you can buy from seed catalogs or garden supply stores.

Beans, beets, cabbage, carrots, onions, peas, greens, squash and tomatoes can be dried.

Where to go to . . .

PRESERVE FOOD

www.uga.edu/nchfp/—A very complete site with a self-paced preservation course.

www.howstuffworks.com—Search for food preservation and be connected with a multitude of links.

www.preservefood.com—Good basic information; offers Master Food Preserver Certificate.

Putting Food By, Janet Greene, Ruth Hertzberg and Beatrice Vaughn, Penguin Books—Complete information on preserving food.

❧ *Save Money and Live Well* ❧

The benefits of growing a garden go far beyond the financial returns, but let's start there anyway. It's hard to figure out the exact yield of a garden because of all the variables involved, but on average, you can expect the following: One tomato plant yields between four and 25 pounds, depending on the type of tomato; two cucumber plants produce 16 pounds; a 25 foot row of pole beans yields 30 pounds; a 25 foot row of summer squash produces 40 pounds. Prices at the grocery store vary, but as of this writing, the average price for a pound of organic tomatoes is $3.99 a pound. That means that if you planted just one tomato plant, you would have saved an average of $39.00, less the cost of the seeds. That's no small potatoes!

But wait—there's more. Gardening saves you money on gas because you don't have to drive to the store for that salad and on entertainment because you're spending your FREE time having fun in the garden.

And of course there are the priceless benefits of growing your own vegetables. You don't have to worry about whether chemicals are tainting your food. You get to be out in nature. Your garden becomes a family project that binds you together. And you can feel good about saving the planet because you're helping to cut down the pollution and the use of fossil fuels that result from shipping produce from one state to another.

REFLECTING AND PROJECTING

When the first hard frost comes and the growing season is over, you might feel like your gardening work is done, but you still have at least one more thing to do before you close down your garden. Pull up any branches or leaves that look diseased and throw them out. You can leave the remains of the healthy plants in the ground and wait until next spring to turn them over into the soil or pull them up. If you're feeling especially motivated, dig up your garden in the fall and plant a cover crop of winter rye, clover, vetch, alfalfa or another plant that keeps weeds out while it nourishes the soil. When you chop it up and turn it into the soil in the spring, it will enrich your garden plot. The seed catalogs listed on page 6 sell cover crops. Finally, make yourself a note to remember to rotate the crops in your garden next year.

Rotating crops is the practice of planting specific crops in different places in the garden every year in order to avoid diseases. Rotating crops is essential if you want to have a disease-free garden.

Now it's time to stop for a minute and look at all you've done. "Give yourself a pat on the back," as my math teacher used to say to us if we did well on a test. You've proven to yourself that you have what it takes to be a gardener. You had the opportunity to see a seed turn into your supper. You saved money and you had fun—and this is only the beginning. Wait until you see next year's garden!

REFERENCES AND RESOURCES

My book, *Digging It*, is a basic guide for gardening. If you get bitten by the gardening bug and want to get more detailed information, here are some resources for you:

❧ *Books* ☙

The Book of Outdoor Gardening, Smith and Hawken, Workman Publishing Company, ISBN 0-7611-0110-1—Complete coverage of how to plant and care for many types of gardens and detailed descriptions of a large variety of plants and flowers.

The Complete Guide to Herbs—A Practical Guide to Growing and Using Herbs, Lesley Bremmers, Viking Studio, ISBN 0-14-02-3802-6— You could survive with this as your only book on herbs. Fantastic.

From the Ground Up, The Story of a First Garden, Amy Stewart, St. Martin's Griffin Publishing, ISBN 0-312-28767-4—An enjoyable memoir for gardeners to read as they experience their own gardening adventure.

Gardening—The Complete Guide to Growing America's Favorite Fruits and Vegetables, National Gardening Association, Addison-Wesley Publishing, ISBN 0-201-10855-0—An outstanding resource with detailed information on every aspect of vegetable and fruit gardening.

The Guide to Self-Sufficiency, John Seymour, Hearst Books, ISBN 0-910990-74-3—Goes way beyond vegetable gardening with directions for starting and sustaining a self-supporting homestead/farm.

The New Victory Garden by Bob Thomson, Little Brown Publishing, ISBN 0-316-84337-7—Extensive information on vegetable gardening month by month from the host of the PBS Victory Garden show. Includes detailed instructions on making compost bins, cold frames, trellises and other garden structures.

⅏ *Web Sites* ⅏

Visit *www.urbanfarming.org* to learn about and share garden tips, as well as tips on healthy eating, healthy recipes, healthy fitness, healthy finances, healthy families, green collar job training opportunities and more on the social forum. You may also register your garden and be a part of the *Urban Farming Global Food Chain*®!

www.csrees.usda.gov/Extension/—A guide to every extension office in the U.S.

www.eartheasy.com—A green living web site with very good articles about gardening.

webgarden.osu.edu—Links to all the information you could want about gardening.

⅏ *Short List of Commonly Used Terms* ⅏

Annual—Plants that go through their entire life cycle in one season.

Balanced Fertilizer—A fertilizer that contains an equal percentage of nitrogen, phosphorus and potassium *(NPK)*. A label for this fertilizer might be 10-10-10.

Biennial—Plants that grow for two years. The first year they grow and put out leaves, but they usually don't flower or fruit until the second year, and after that, they die.

Frost Dates—The days of the last frost in the spring and first frost in the fall based on zones.

Companion Planting—The practice of planting certain crops together that help each other improve growth and discourage disease.

Germination Mix—A light, soil-type product that allows seeds to establish roots easily.

Hardening off—Process of exposing seedlings to the outdoors a little at a time so they'll thrive when they're planted in the ground.

Perennial—Plants that die back in the winter but come back again and get bigger year after year.

Rotating Crops—The practice of planting specific crops in different places in the garden every year in order to avoid diseases.

Row Cover—Light material used to cover plants to protect them from insects and from the cold.

Side Dress—To put granular fertilizer around the stem of the plant and work it into the soil.

Succession Planting—The practice of planting one crop in the same spot as another as soon as the first crop matures.

Thin—To pull out any seedlings that are growing closer than the recommended spacing on the seed packet.

Vermiculite—A white mica substance that retains water and releases it at a later time.

True leaves—Second set of leaves that your seedling grows, and that have the same shape as the leaves of the mature plant.

Zone—A geographic section of the country, determined by climate as defined by the USDA.

❧ Notes ❧

Made in the USA
Columbia, SC
14 June 2020